Artful Botanical Embroidery

Artful Botanical Embroidery
First Published in 2023 by Zakka Workshop,
a division of World Book Media, LLC

www.zakkaworkshop.com
134 Federal Street
Salem, MA 01970
info@zakkaworkshop.com

SHISHU DE EGAKU SHOKUBUTSU MOYO (NV70671)
Copyright ©2022 Alice Makabe/NIHON VOGUE-SHA.
All rights reserved.
Originally published in Japanese language by
NIHON VOGUE Corp.
English language rights, translation & production by
World Book Media, LLC

Photography: Yukari Shirai
Editor: Jun Sasaki
Styling: Megumi Nishimori
Book Design: Motoko Kitsukawa
Tracing: Yumiko Matsumoto
Copy Editor: Sakae Suzuki
Translation: Kyoko Matthews
English Editor: Lindsay Fair

ISBN: 978-1-940552-75-0

Printed in China

10 9 8 7 6 5 4 3 2 1

About the Author

Alice Makabe is an embroidery
artist from Tokyo. She holds
embroidery workshops and
exhibitions and is the author of
Beautiful Botanical Embroidery.
She makes an effort to stitch
every day as a way to capture
the special moments and joy
of the season. Visit her website
at makabealice.jimdofree.com
and find her on Instagram
@alice_makabe.

Artful Botanical Embroidery

A Collection of
32 Patterns & Projects
for All Seasons

ALICE MAKABE

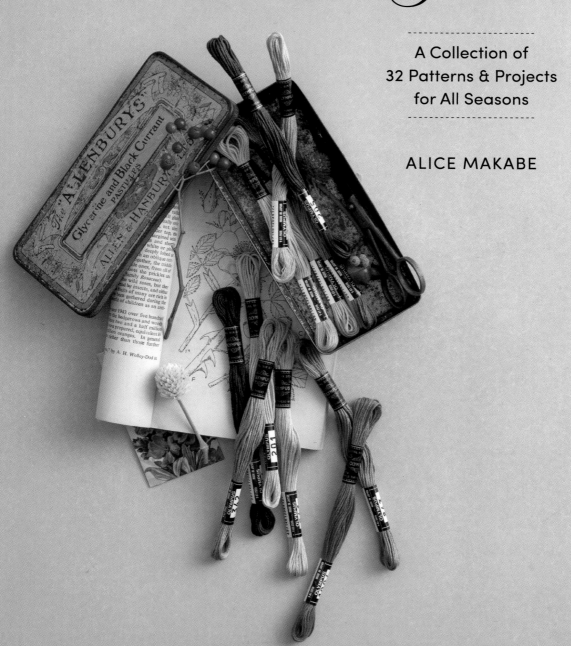

Contents

Autumn

17 ···24

18 ···25

19 ···26

20 ···27

21 ···28

22 ···29

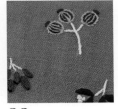

23 ···30

24 ···31

Winter

25 ···32

26 ···33

27 ···34

28 ···35

29 ···36

30 ···37

31 ···38

32 ···39

Before You Begin

Introduction

I can still clearly remember the floral pattern on my favorite sundress that I wore as a young child—it had rows of small flowers with lines in between them that reminded me of waves. I never tired of that pattern and its perfect symmetry.

Later on in life, I traveled to India and was awestruck by the beautiful saris worn by the women I saw there. To my surprise, the intricate patterns printed on those colorful fabrics were actually consecutive repeats of simple motifs. Each motif was simple on its own, but when repeated, produced a stunning rhythmic pattern printed on soft fabric.

If you take a look around, you'll be amazed at how many patterns we encounter in our daily lives. Inspired by the patterns all around me, I created this book to explore and celebrate them through floral embroidery.

Organized by season, you'll find soft, muted motifs to embroider in springtime, refreshing patterns for summer, warm, rich color combinations for autumn and bold, vivid hues to brighten up the winter.

A single motif can be used to create a nearly endless number of patterns, just by changing the color scheme or orientation. I hope these designs inspire you to stitch your own favorite floral patterns for years to come.

—Alice Makabe

Spring

When you start to feel a warm
breeze in the air, it's time for the flowers
to awaken. Let's use soft colors of
embroidery floss to capture the first
blooms of spring. Welcome the arrival of
the season with each stitch as you create
patterns of fresh leaves, petals, and
stems dancing together in the wind.

01 & 02

Create a border pattern by arranging small flowers that are just starting to bud in early spring. I stitched the design on the opposite page onto yellow linen because it reminds me of warm sunshine. This L-shaped design is also perfect for a rectangular placemat, as shown in the pink and green color scheme above. Simply adjust the number of repeats to change the size or shape.

Embroidery motif 01 on page 60 • Embroidery motif and project 02 on page 61

03　Violets are the first flower that come to mind when I think of spring. Use this sweet motif on its own or arrange consecutive motifs to create a pattern.

Embroidery motif on page 63

04

Little violet bouquets are stitched onto gingham check fabric in this fashionable spring purse. It's fun to think about all of the combinations that can be created by pairing patterned fabric with embroidery—it's almost like designing textiles.

Instructions on page 64

05 Small flowers bloom in oval-shaped frames. Ten different designs are shown here, but you could stitch a single design in different colors or repeat just two or three designs.

Embroidery motif on page 67

06 Use these mini motifs individually for elegant floral brooches.
I opted for contrasting color background fabric to make the
embroidery motifs stand out.

Instructions on page 68

07 Swallows fly in an arc as they make nests for their new families. Embroider the eyes on top of the white portions of the face to really make them pop.

Embroidery motif on page 69

08 This oval-shaped design is composed of flowers and leaves gently swaying in the breeze. Just two shades of green embroidery floss are used here, but you can incorporate additional colors for a bolder look.

Embroidery motif on page 70

Summer

Under the strong rays of the sun and soaking rain from thunderstorms, plants grow quickly in the summertime. Use bright, beautiful colors to stitch up these summer-inspired floral patterns.

09 & 10

Inspired by a summer day at the ocean, I drew the underwater scene on the opposite page featuring colorful seaweed and coral. For a more subtle look, use pale silver gray floss to stitch the same motif on blue linen as seen above. Tied with rope, this drawstring bag possesses a slightly nautical look.

Embroidery motif 09 on page 71 • Embroidery motif and project 10 on page 72

11   Stitched on crisp white fabric, these blue embroidery
motifs are reminiscent of hand-painted tiles. Each
design is a square, so they can be aligned horizontally
or vertically.

Embroidery motif on page 75

12

Here, the motifs from the opposite page are arranged vertically to create a decorative wall hanging. This color scheme was inspired by terracotta tiles, and offers an earthy, neutral look.

Instructions on page 76

13 I am constantly sketching leaves and flowers in various notebooks. Later, I'll combine them to create pretty embroidery patterns. Here, I used assorted shades of green to depict the lushness of the hot summer season.

Embroidery motif on page 79

14   Use your favorite motifs to embellish small sachets, which can be filled with lavender to keep your linens fresh. Intentionally place the embroidery design off-center to create a lively impression.

Instructions on page 80

15

This large-scale retro floral pattern would be perfect for embroidering on a summer sundress or peasant top.

Embroidery motif on page 83

16 Try stitching up the same motif in a cool pastel color scheme for a softer look. Have fun experimenting with alternative color combinations to create different impressions using the same design.

Embroidery motif on page 84

Autumn

Autumn flowers begin to bloom as the days grow shorter and the air turns crisp. These flowers display rich, bold colors and beautiful shapes.

17 & 18

On the opposite page, a two-tone pattern is embroidered on dark brown linen for an eye-catching motif. The simple little bag above features the same motif stitched in a cocoa color scheme. Pink fabric can tend to look juvenile, but when paired with soft brown embroidery floss, it creates a chic, mature look.

Embroidery motif 17 on page 85 • Embroidery motif and project 18 on page 86

19 This autumn sampler is composed of a collection of motifs that can be repeated to create linear border designs or combined in a nearly endless number of possibilities.

Embroidery motif on page 89

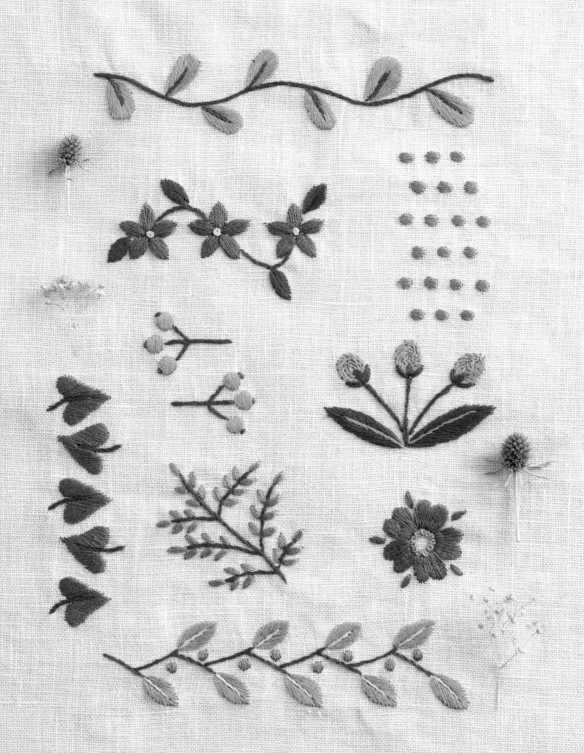

20 Use the motifs from the opposite page to embellish a patchwork clutch. Embroider large pieces of fabric in a hoop, then trim to size and sew together to make this eclectic accessory.

Instructions on page 90

21 Tiny floral motifs are aligned to create a continuous pattern inspired by the gorgeous Provencal fabrics of southern France. Here, bullion stitch is used for the petals to produce a three-dimensional effect.

Embroidery motif on page 93

22

For an understated look, stitch the floral motifs in the same color floss as the fabric. A slightly shiny satin fabric was used to create an elegant drawstring bag perfect for a special event.

Instructions on page 94

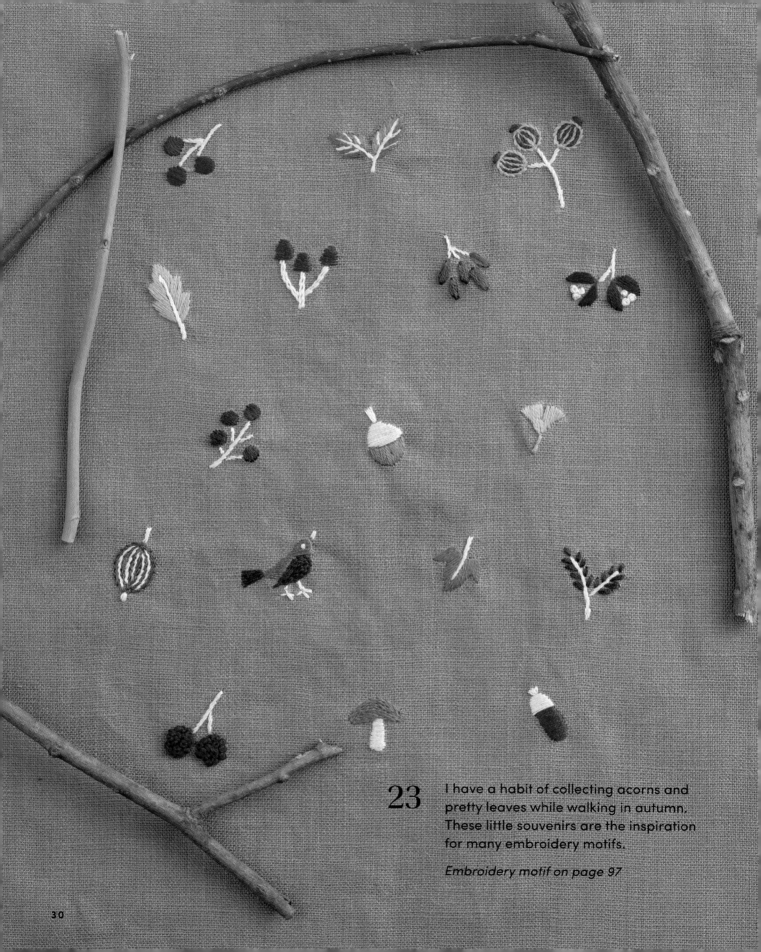

23 I have a habit of collecting acorns and pretty leaves while walking in autumn. These little souvenirs are the inspiration for many embroidery motifs.

Embroidery motif on page 97

24 These small-scale motifs are the ideal size to embroider on the corner of a napkin or handkerchief. You can even combine a few designs to create your own little story stitched in floss.

Instructions on page 98

Winter

Winter is the perfect time of year for vivid colors and bold patterns. A colorful floral print dress I saw at a party, a red floral bag reflecting against a snowy backdrop— these motifs were inspired by the sights of the season.

25 & 26

Whenever I see flowers blooming during the coldest season of the year, it instantly elevates my mood. On the opposite page, red and black embroidery floss on snowy white linen creates a fresh, clean look as clear and as crisp as the winter air. Change out the embroidery floss and linen colors to create a cooler impression. Above, the same floral motif shown on page 32 is stitched on a simple zippered pouch, and then adapted into a circular design for a pin cushion.

Embroidery motif 25 on page 99 • Embroidery motif and project 26 on page 100

27   Vivid floral embroidery creates a striking impression against a black backdrop. We tend to spend the most time at home during the winter, so I made this small panel to enjoying looking at while indoors.

Embroidery motif on page 103

28 With assorted blooming flowers and a little bird on a branch, this unique tree is the perfect motif to embroider while you wait for spring's arrival.

Embroidery motif on page 104

29

Experiment with color and texture by stitching these beautiful flower samplers. Use two contrasting colors as shown here, or opt for a more vibrant palette.

Embroidery motifs on pages 105 and 106

30

Although these bookmarks are small, they are a wonderful canvas for floral embroidery. Stitch one up and give it as a gift to an avid reader in your life.

Instructions on page 107

31 Inspired by the colors of a winter evening, shades of blue
embroidery floss are paired with dark blue linen to create a quiet
nighttime garden scene.

Embroidery motif on page 110

32

Red and white is a classic embroidery color scheme for good reason—it brightens the room and creates a lovely, warm feeling. This motif is designed to be mounted in a 8" embroidery hoop.

Embroidery motif on page 111

Before You Begin

Tools & Materials

In the following guide, I'll introduce the tools and materials I used to stitch the designs in this book.

① Embroidery floss

The designs in this book were stitched with No. 25 embroidery floss, which is the most common weight of embroidery floss and is offered in a wide variety of colors. This type of floss is composed of six easily separated strands. Change the number of strands used to alter the thickness of the finished stitch. Olympus brand floss was used to stitch the designs in this book. A conversion chart for DMC brand is included on page 59.

② Linen fabric

The majority of the projects in this book were stitched on linen fabric, which is available in assorted colors and weights. Choose the color and fabric weight based on the finished use of the embroidery project. Wash the fabric and adhere fusible interfacing to the wrong side before embroidering (refer to page 48).

③ Cotton/rayon satin

In addition to linen fabric, cotton and cotton blend fabrics can also be used for embroidery. The fabric pictured here is a cotton/rayon blend and was used for project 22 on page 29. Because this fabric is a tightly woven satin with a slightly shiny finish, it is not necessary to adhere fusible interfacing to the wrong side before embroidering.

④ Cotton gingham

Print fabrics can also be used for embroidery, such as this cotton gingham used in project 4 on page 11. Light colored print fabrics will be easier to work with when transferring the embroidery design. For best results, make sure that the scale of the print matches the embroidery motif.

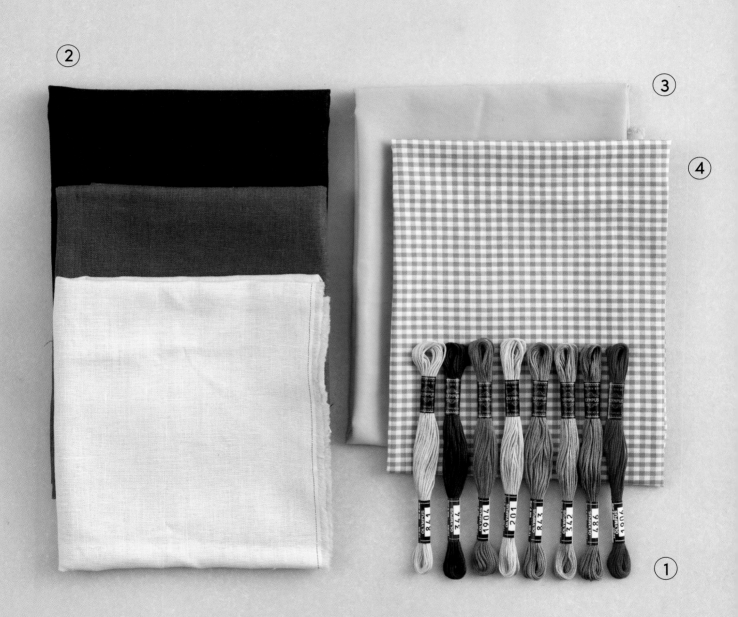

① Fusible interfacing

Adhere fusible interfacing to the wrong side of the linen fabric before embroidering to prevent it from distorting or shrinking. Don't use fusible interfacing if the wrong side of the fabric will be visible on the finished project, such as on a handkerchief or napkin. Thin, woven fusible interfacing will work well for the projects in this book. **Note:** Make sure to adhere the fusible interfacing before transferring the embroidery motif onto the fabric so that you don't accidentally smear or erase the lines.

② Scissors

You'll need a pair of fabric shears to cut linen fabric and a pair of fine, sharp thread snips to cut embroidery floss. Craft scissors are handy for cutting leather, felt, and other thick materials.

③ Embroidery hoop

A 4"–5" (10–12 cm) diameter embroidery hoop will work well for the majority of the designs in this book. Wrap the inner hoop with a bias strip to help hold the fabric taut during stitching.

④ Transfer papers

Use tracing paper to copy an embroidery design from the book, then use cellophane and carbon chalk paper to transfer the embroidery design onto fabric using the process shown on page 49.

⑤ Tracer pen, pencil, and ruler

Use a sharp pencil, such as a mechanical pencil, to copy the embroidery design onto tracing paper. Next, use a tracer pen (or empty ballpoint pen) to transfer the copied embroidery design onto linen fabric using the process shown on page 49. Use a ruler to draw straight lines on the fabric or to measure the size of the design.

⑥ Needles, threader, and pins

Use French embroidery needles with sharp points. A needle threader is helpful for inserting the embroidery floss through the eye of the needle. Use pins to hold the layers in place while transferring the design onto fabric and while constructing projects.

A Note on Embroidery Needles

French embroidery needles were used to stitch the projects in this book. These needles feature sharply pointed tips and wide eyes that make threading easier. French embroidery needles are available in various sizes—select the appropriate size based on the number of strands of embroidery floss used, as well as the thickness of the fabric.

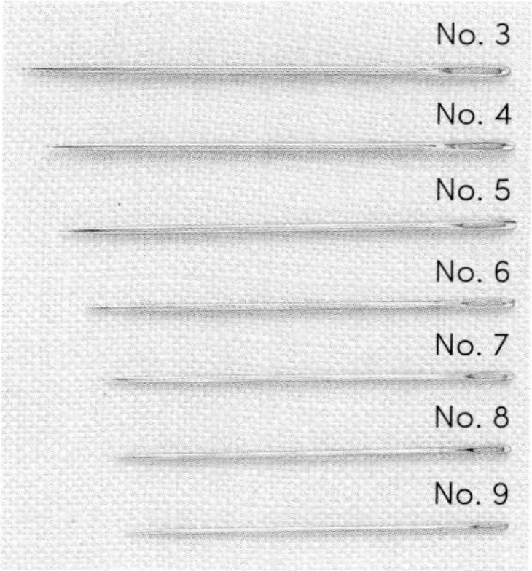

No. 3
No. 4
No. 5
No. 6
No. 7
No. 8
No. 9

The size numbers listed in the photo at left and chart below feature Clover Gold Eye embroidery needles. Needle size numbers and thicknesses vary by manufacturer. **Note:** The image shows the needles at full-size.

Needle Size	No. 25 Embroidery Floss Strands
No. 3	6 strands or more
No. 4	5–6 strands
No. 5	4–5 strands
No. 6	3–4 strands
No. 7	2–3 strands
No. 8	1–2 strands
No. 9	1 strand

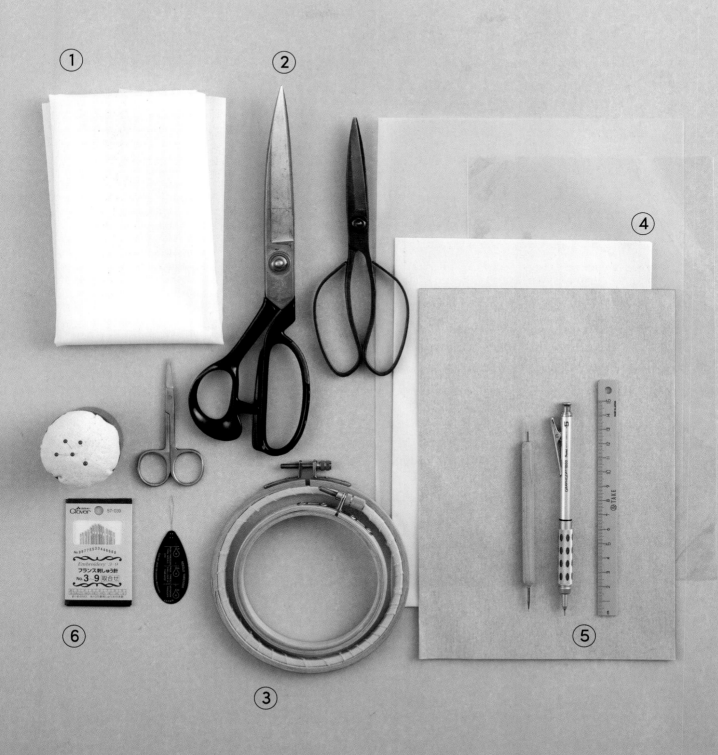

Getting Started

Before you can start embroidering, you'll need to prepare your threads and fabric and transfer the embroidery design. Use the following techniques to get set up for successful embroidery.

Prepare the Embroidery Floss

Use this handy technique to prepare a skein of embroidery floss into easy to manage lengths for stitching.

1. Remove the labels from the skein of floss. The floss should be wound into a loop.

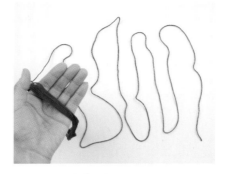

2. Unwind the loop into one long piece. It will measure about 8¾ yards (8 m). Fold the entire length in half, aligning the beginning and end of the floss.

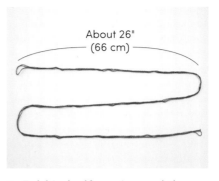

3. Fold in half again, and then fold into three equal parts.

4. Gather the bundle of floss together, then cut the loops at both ends. This will create twelve lengths of thread about 26" (66 cm) each.

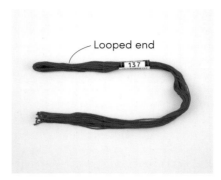

5. Fold the bundle in half. Thread the label noting the color number back onto the looped end.

6. Use the needle to separate individual strands of thread from the looped end of the bundle.

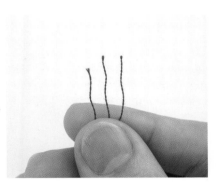

Tip

Always separate the individual strands of embroidery floss, even if you plan to stitch with all six. This will help to achieve smooth and tidy stitches and prevent the floss from tangling.

7. Realign the required number of strands once they have been separated.

Thread the Needle

Insert the embroidery floss through the eye of the needle using this easy technique. You can also use a needle threader.

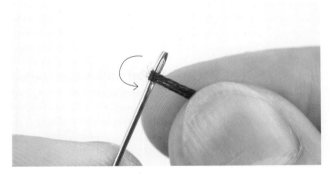

1. Wrap the embroidery floss around the eye of the needle and pull to form a crease.

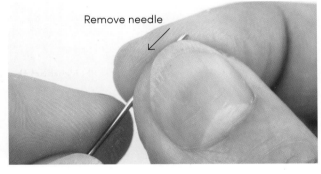

Remove needle

2. Pinch the eye of the needle between your fingers to flatten the floss, then pull the needle down to remove it.

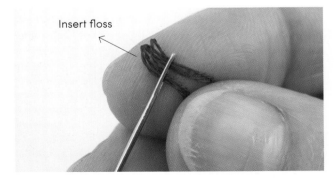

Insert floss

3. Insert the flattened floss through the eye of the needle.

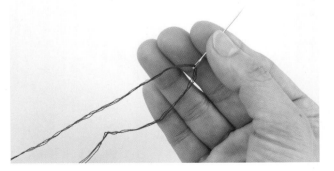

4. Pull the floss through the eye of the needle so that the needle is about 4" (10 cm) from the crease.

Prewash Your Fabric

It's important to prewash your fabric before you start embroidering, especially if you plan to make the embroidery into an item that will be washed frequently, such as an apron or kitchen towel. To prewash, soak the fabric in water for about an hour. Smooth out the wrinkles and let the fabric dry without squeezing or wringing it out. Before the fabric dries completely, press with an iron, adjusting the fabric grain if necessary.

Adhere Fusible Interfacing

Adhere fusible interfacing to the wrong side of the fabric before transferring the embroidery design. This will prevent puckering while stitching.

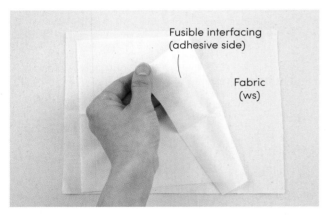

1. Cut the fusible interfacing slightly larger than the embroidery design. Align the adhesive surface (rough side) of the fusible interfacing with the wrong side of the fabric.

2. Press with the iron for 10–15 seconds. Use the appropriate heat setting based on the type of fabric.

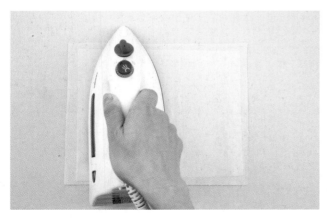

3. Pick up the iron and move it to press the embroidery design in small increments.

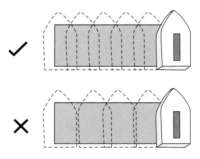

4. Make sure that the ironed areas overlap slightly as shown in the diagram above. Do not glide the iron back and forth over the entire area. Lay the fabric flat until cool to the touch.

Transfer the Embroidery Design

Accurately tracing the design onto the fabric is the first step in creating beautiful embroidery.

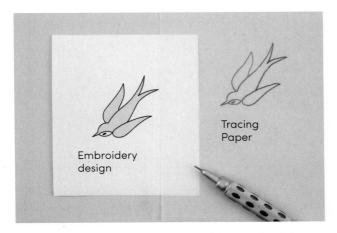

1. Align tracing paper on top of the embroidery design and trace the image using a mechanical pencil. **Note:** It may help to trace or photocopy the embroidery design from the book onto a flat sheet of paper first.

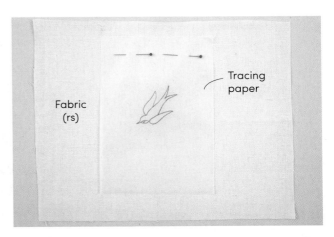

2. Align the tracing paper from step 1 on top of the fabric. Pin in place.

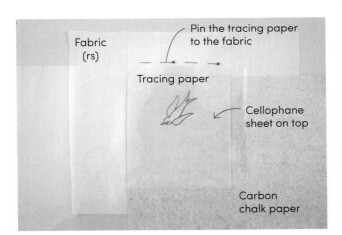

3. Insert a sheet of carbon chalk paper between the fabric and tracing paper. Make sure the chalk side is facing down so it's positioned against the fabric. Align a sheet of cellophane on top of the tracing paper.

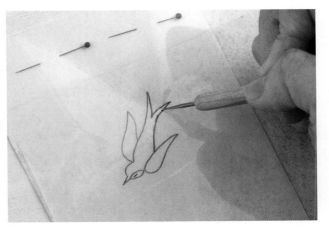

4. Trace the embroidery design using a tracer pen. The pressure of the pen will transfer the chalk from the carbon paper onto the fabric. The cellophane will prevent the tracing paper from ripping, allowing you to reuse it again in the future.

5. Make sure that all the lines have transferred onto the fabric, and then remove all the papers.

6. If necessary, use a fabric pencil to fill in or darken missing lines.

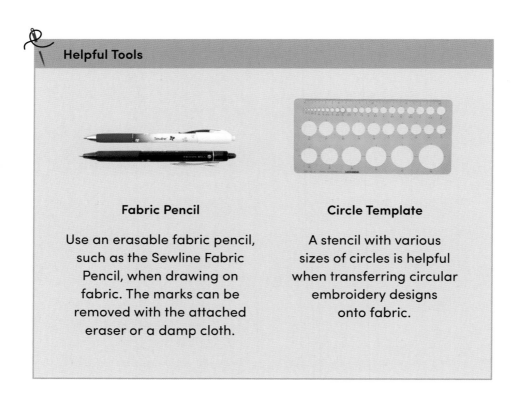

Helpful Tools

Fabric Pencil

Use an erasable fabric pencil, such as the Sewline Fabric Pencil, when drawing on fabric. The marks can be removed with the attached eraser or a damp cloth.

Circle Template

A stencil with various sizes of circles is helpful when transferring circular embroidery designs onto fabric.

Insert Fabric Into Embroidery Hoop

An embroidery hoop will hold your fabric taut during stitching and prevent puckering. If your fabric starts to sag while stitching, stop and tighten the hoop before continuing.

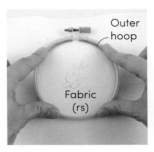

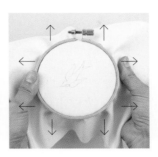

1. Loosen the screw on the outer hoop to release the inner hoop. Align the fabric on top of the inner hoop.

2. Make sure the embroidery design is centered in the hoop, and then fit the outer hoop over the fabric.

3. Gently tug the fabric in all four directions to make sure the fabric grain is aligned at a 90 degree angle.

4. Tighten the screw to pull the fabric taut inside the hoop.

How to Start Stitching

Take care to secure your thread in a neat manner when you first start stitching. This is important for durability, as well as the finished look.

Insert the needle through the right side of the fabric, about 1½" (3–4 cm) from the starting point. Leave a 4" (10 cm) thread tail on the right side of the fabric. Next, draw the needle out at the starting point and start stitching the embroidery design. Be careful not to pull the thread tail through the fabric as you stitch—it will be finished once the stitching is complete.

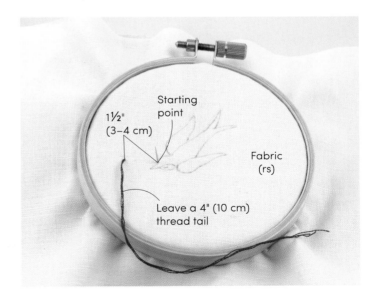

How to Finish Stitching

Take the time to finish your thread ends properly on the wrong side of the fabric, as this will influence the appearance of the embroidery on the right side and ensure your work holds up over time.

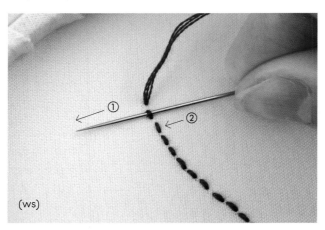

1. Draw the needle out on the wrong side of the fabric. Insert the needle through the back of 2–3 stitches all from the same direction to secure the thread end.

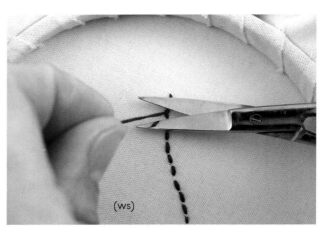

2. Pull the thread taut, then trim the end close to the surface of the fabric.

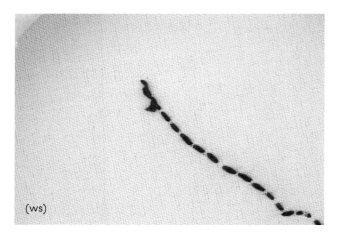

3. Be careful not to pull the stitches too tightly and take care not to insert the needle through to the right side of the fabric.

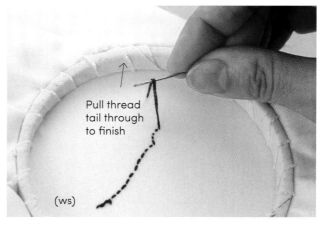

Pull thread tail through to finish

4. Pull the thread tail left when you started stitching through to the wrong side of the fabric. Thread it onto the needle and secure using the same process shown in steps 1 and 2.

Alternative Method

Use this option for starting and finishing threads when the thread end can be hidden under the embroidery stitches, such as when working satin stitch or long and short stitch, as shown below.

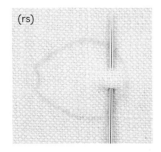

1. Make a small stitch inside the embroidery design from the right side of the fabric.

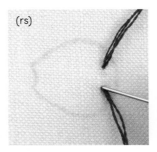

2. Make a backstitch by inserting the needle back through the same hole where you first inserted the needle in step 1. Leave a thread tail.

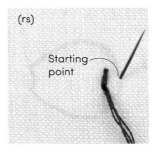

3. Make sure to hold the backstitch and thread tail in place as you pull the thread through the fabric. Next, draw the needle out at the starting point along the traced embroidery design.

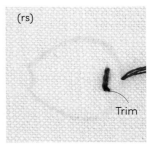

4. Trim the thread tail close to the surface of the fabric. Additional embroidery stitches will be worked on top, so this will not be visible in the finished work.

5. Work the designated embroidery stitches to fill the embroidery design and cover the backstitch. When the embroidery is complete, insert the needle through the back of 2–3 stitches on the wrong side of the fabric.

6. Pull the thread through, then insert the needle under an additional 2–3 stitches to secure.

7. Take care not to insert the needle through to the right side of the fabric when securing the thread. Trim the excess thread close to the surface of the fabric.

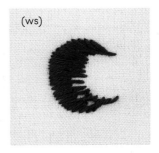

8. Completed view of the finished thread.

Finishing Your Embroidery

Make sure to remove any stray chalk marks from your fabric before ironing; otherwise, the heat of the iron can set the marks in place.

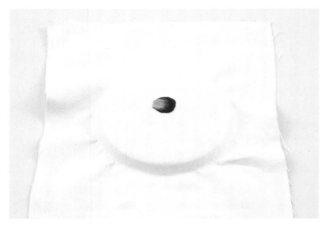

1. Once the embroidery is complete, remove the fabric from the hoop.

2. Use a wet cotton swab to gently remove any stray chalk marks from the fabric.

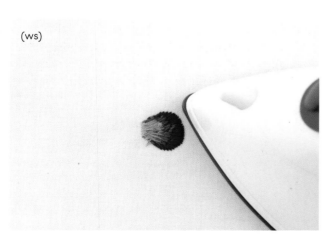

(ws)

3. On the wrong side of the fabric, use the tip of the iron to press the area where the mark was removed, taking care to avoid the embroidered area.

> **Tip**
>
> As a final finishing step, use a spray bottle to mist the fabric with water, then pull the fabric to adjust the grain, before hanging it to dry.

Embroidery Techniques

The following techniques utilize basic embroidery stitches to create beautiful, interesting effects perfect for botanical embroidery.

STRAIGHT STITCH INSIDE OF LAZY DAISY

This technique is often used to stitch petals and small leaves. Work from the base of the petal or leaf toward the tip to create a three-dimensional finish.

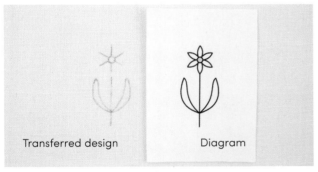

1. The diagrams in the book will show the finished shape of the embroidery design, but for best results with this stitch, I recommend using only a straight line to mark the length of petals when transferring the design onto fabric. This will produce a neater finished work.

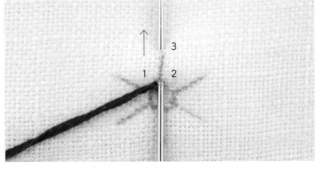

2. Start by making a lazy daisy stitch: Draw the needle out at 1, insert the needle at 2, and draw it out again at 3.

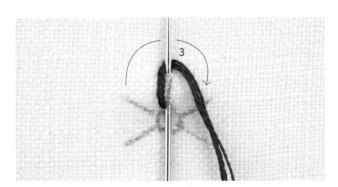

3. Wrap the thread around the needle. Pull the thread taut.

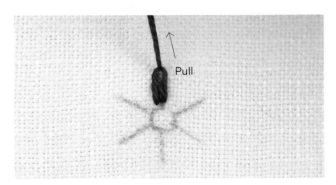

4. Pull the needle and thread out of the fabric to draw the loop closed.

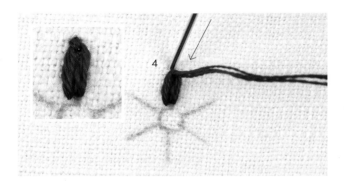

5. Make a small straight stitch (4) to secure the loop in place. The lazy daisy stitch is now complete.

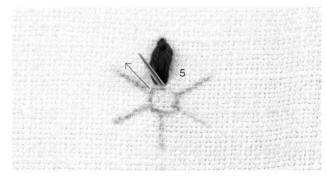

6. Next, you'll fill the center of the loop with a straight stitch. Draw the needle out at the base of the lazy daisy stitch (5, which is also the same hole as 1).

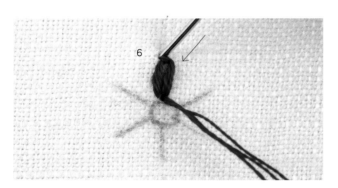

7. Insert the needle 6 (which is also the same hole as 4).

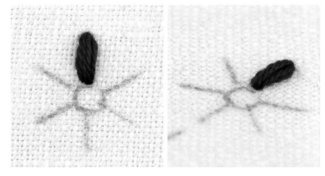

8. The straight stitch is now complete. Take care not to pull the straight stitch too tight.

LONG AND SHORT STITCH

Some may find long and short stitch difficult, but it is actually easier to fill large areas with this stitch than with satin stitch. For best results, divide the area to be filled into sections and work each section starting from the center.

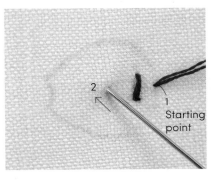

1. Refer to steps 1–4 on page 53 to secure the thread for long and short stitch. Draw the thread out at the starting point (1) and make a long stitch for the first stitch (2).

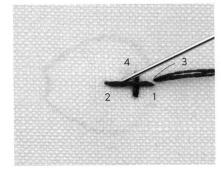

2. Draw the needle out along the traced embroidery design just next to starting point (3). Next, make a shorter stitch (4) that is about half the length of the long stitch you just made.

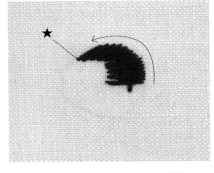

3. Repeat this process to fill half of the first section of the embroidery design, alternating long and short stitches. The ★ symbol indicates the position to insert the needle after completing half of the first section.

4. Insert the needle through the stitches on the wrong side of the fabric to return to the center (starting point). Do not cut the thread.

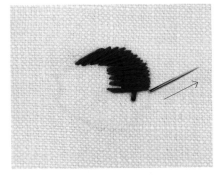

5. Draw the needle out along the traced embroidery design just next to the first long stitch, as in step 2. You will now stitch the other half of the first section of the embroidery design working from the center outward.

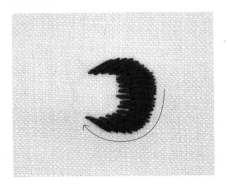

6. Follow the same process used in steps 2 and 3 to fill the space using alternating long and short stitches. When it's time to change floss colors, finish the thread as shown in steps 5–8 on page 53.

7. Secure the new thread by inserting the needle under a few stitches from the first section on the wrong side of the fabric.

8. Start stitching the second section, working from the center outward. Align each stitch for this second section between two long stitches from the first section.

9. Make all the stitches in the second section an equal length to fill the gaps between the long and short stitches of the first section.

10. Half of the second section is now complete. Make your stitches in a fan shape so that the stitches spread out rather than overlapping.

11. Follow the same process shown in step 4 to insert the needle under the stitches on the wrong side of the fabric and return to the center. Next, fill the other half of the second section following the same process used in steps 9 and 10.

12. Use the same process shown in steps 7–11 to fill the third section with equal length stitches. Finish the thread as shown in steps 5–8 on page 53.

Project Instructions

Here you'll find some helpful information on reading the embroidery templates, as well as an embroidery floss conversion chart.

A Note on How to Read Embroidery Diagrams

The embroidery diagrams contain all the information you'll need to stitch the designs in this book. The following guide shows how to read the embroidery diagrams. Above each embroidery diagram, you'll also find some general notes that apply to the entire design.

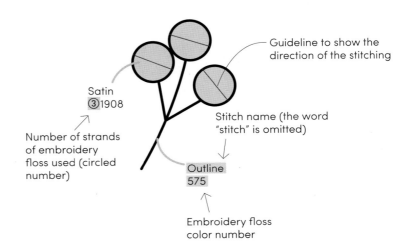

Guideline to show the direction of the stitching

Satin
③ 1908

Number of strands of embroidery floss used (circled number)

Stitch name (the word "stitch" is omitted)

Outline
575

Embroidery floss color number

Thread Conversion Chart

The floss used in this book is Olympus, a popular brand in Japan that is also available worldwide. If you would like to use DMC floss, here is a conversion chart for colors used for the projects in this book.

OLYMPUS	DMC	OLYMPUS	DMC	OLYMPUS	DMC	OLYMPUS	DMC
137	915	316	924	632	3042	841	822
145	349	318	939	654	597	843	612
192	498	341	927	655	550	900	310
194	815	342	926	712	921	1029	814
198	902	343	924	738	801	1035	347
201	504	344	924	741	842	1601	316
202	503	386	517	744	3863	1904	3687
203	502	412	648	755	921	1906	3685
205	520	421	3024	758	920	2013	469
214	470	430	3024	778	838	2014	937
218	469	484	415	783	922	2042	597
222	992	485	318	785	976	2051	3363
244	368	486	414	791	225	2835	832
284	732	488	413	792	225	3040	928
288	3012	563	3045	793	316	3041	927
290	165	575	400	795	221	3042	415
305	517	623	210	810	762	3043	930
314	926	631	3743	811	3024	7020	3866

Full-Size Embroidery Template

- Materials: Olympus No. 25 embroidery floss in 343, 712, 785, 2835, 3042
- Use 2 strands unless otherwise noted
- French knots are wrapped twice
- ★ = Straight stitch inside of lazy daisy

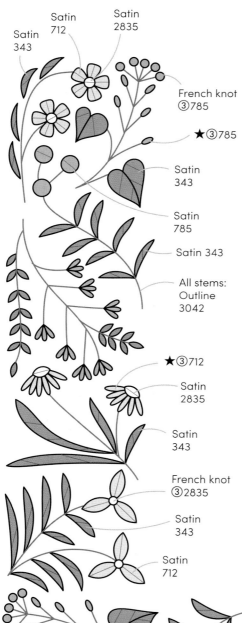

Satin 343

Satin 712

Satin 2835

French knot ③785

★③785

Satin 343

Satin 785

Satin 343

All stems: Outline 3042

★③712

Satin 2835

Satin 343

French knot ③2835

Satin 343

Satin 712

Lazy daisy 785

★343

02

SHOWN ON PAGE 9

Materials

- ½ yard (0.5 m) of white linen fabric
- 18" × 12" (45.5 × 30.5 cm) of fusible interfacing
- Olympus No. 25 embroidery floss in 288, 791, 793, 841, 2013

Construction Steps

Use ⅜" (1 cm) seam allowance unless otherwise specified.

1. Cut a 13" × 16" (33 × 40.5 cm) rectangle of white linen fabric for the front. Mark a 7" × 10" (18 × 25.5 cm) rectangle for the finished size. You will trim the fabric to size after embroidering. Adhere fusible interfacing to the wrong side in the area where the fabric will be embroidered. Transfer the template on page 62 onto this portion of the fabric, following the placement noted below. You will need four repeats total to complete the border design. Embroider as noted.

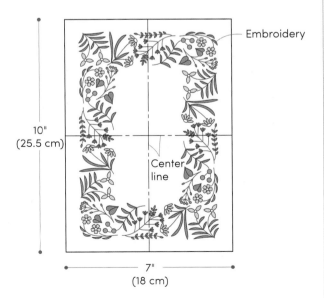

10"
(25.5 cm)

Embroidery

Center line

7"
(18 cm)

2. Trim the embroidered front to 7¾" × 10¾" (20 × 27.5 cm). These dimensions include seam allowance. Cut another rectangle of white linen fabric to this size for the back. Adhere fusible interfacing to the wrong side of the back.

3. Align the front and back with right sides together. Sew together around all four sides, leaving a 2½" (6 cm) opening on one side.

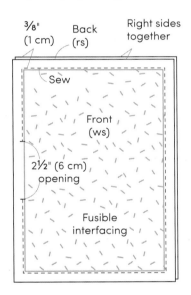

⅜"
(1 cm)

Back
(rs)

Right sides together

Sew

Front
(ws)

2½" (6 cm)
opening

Fusible
interfacing

4. Turn right side out through the opening. Adjust the shape as necessary, making sure the corners appear as crisp points. Hand stitch the opening closed.

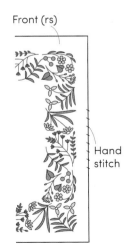

Front (rs)

Hand stitch

Full-Size Embroidery Template

- Use 2 strands unless otherwise noted
- French knots are wrapped twice
- ★ = Straight stitch inside of lazy daisy

Satin 2013

Satin 791

Satin 841

French knot ③793

★③793

Satin 2013

Satin 793

Satin 2013

All stems: Outline 288

★③791

Satin 841

Satin 2013

French knot ③793

Satin 2013

Satin 791

Lazy daisy 793

★2013

03

Full-Size Embroidery Template

- Materials: Olympus No. 25 embroidery floss in 201, 341, 344, 486, 792, 841, 2835
- Use 3 strands unless otherwise noted
- French knots are wrapped twice

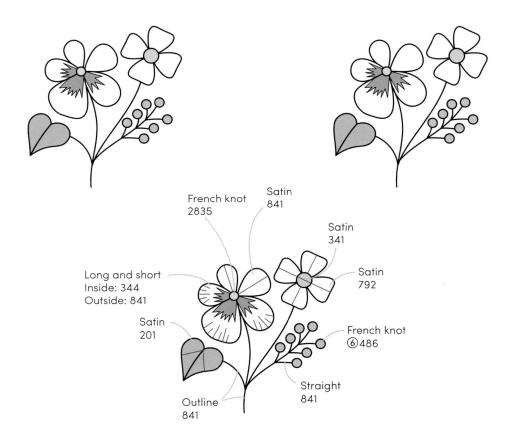

French knot
2835

Satin
841

Satin
341

Long and short
Inside: 344
Outside: 841

Satin
792

Satin
201

French knot
⑥486

Outline
841

Straight
841

04 SHOWN ON PAGE 11

Materials

- ¾ yard (0.5 m) of gray gingham fabric (for the bag outside)
- ½ yard (0.4 m) of cotton fabric (for the lining)
- 31½" × 13¾" (80 x 35 cm) of fusible interfacing
- Olympus No. 25 embroidery floss in 194, 288, 343, 344, 488, 841, 2835

Construction Steps

Use ⅜" (1 cm) seam allowance unless otherwise specified.

1. Cut a 21" × 17¾" (53 x 45 cm) rectangle of gingham fabric for the front. Mark a 15" × 11¾" (38 x 30 cm) rectangle for the finished size. You will trim the fabric to size after embroidering. Adhere fusible interfacing to the wrong side in the area where the fabric will be embroidered. Transfer the template on page 66 onto this portion of the fabric, following the placement noted below. Embroider as noted.

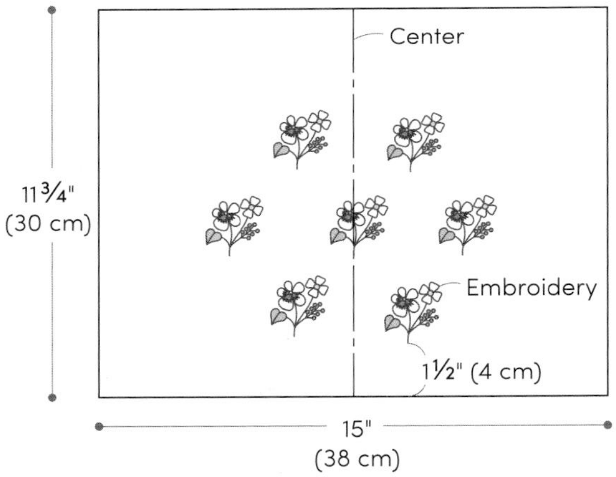

2. Cut two 15¾" × 2" (50 x 5 cm) rectangles of gingham fabric for the handles.

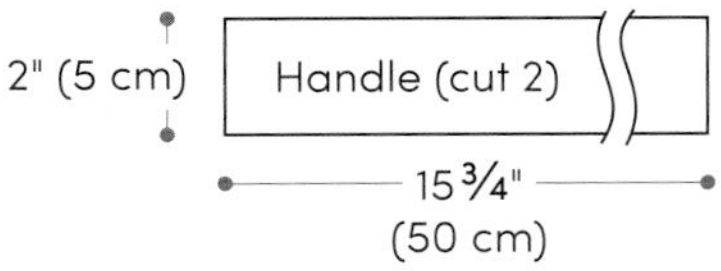

3. To make each handle, fold and press each long edge in ⅜" (1 cm). Then, fold the handle in half and press. Topstitch, stitching as close to the edge as possible.

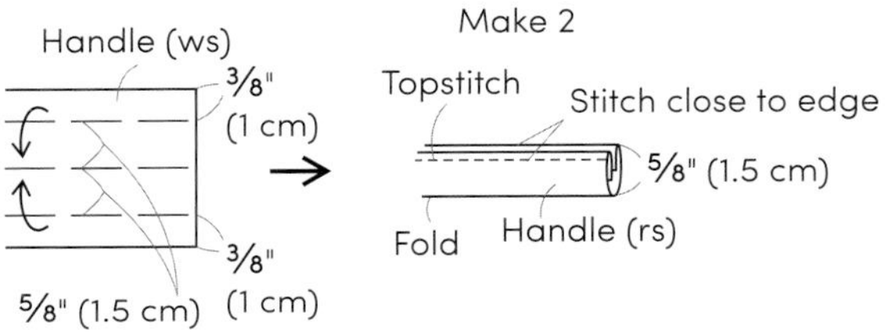

4. Cut two 35½" × 1½" (90 x 4 cm) rectangles of gingham fabric for the drawstring cords.

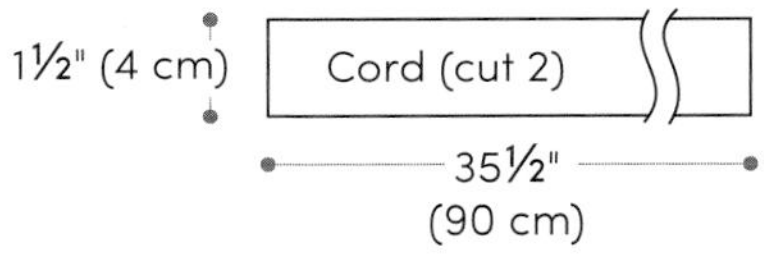

5. To make each drawstring cord, fold and press each short edge in ⅜" (1 cm). Next, fold and press each long edge in ⅜" (1 cm). Finally, fold the cord in half and press. Topstitch, stitching as close to the edge as possible.

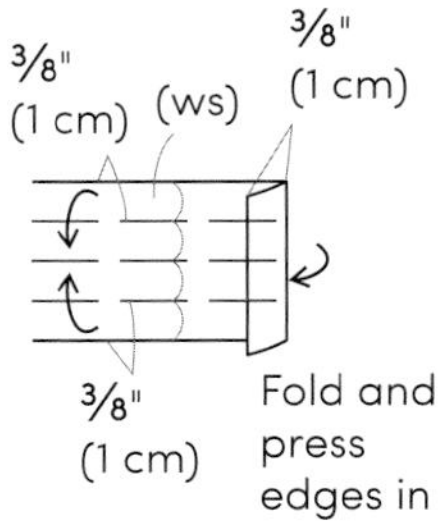

6. Trim the embroidered front to 15¾" × 12½" (40 x 32 cm). These dimensions include seam allowance. Cut another rectangle of gingham fabric to this size for the back. Adhere fusible interfacing to the wrong side. Cut two more rectangles of cotton fabric to this size for the lining.

7. Baste one handle to the right side of the bag front following the placement noted below. Next, align the bag front and one lining with right sides together and sew along the top. Repeat this step with the bag back and remaining handle and lining.

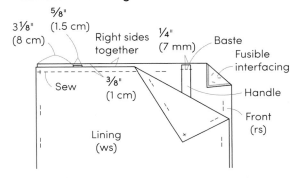

8. Press the seam allowances open. Align the two units from step 7 with right sides together. Sew around all four sides, leaving a 3⅛" (8 cm) opening along the bottom of the lining and ¾" (2 cm) drawstring openings following the placement noted below. Press the seam allowances open.

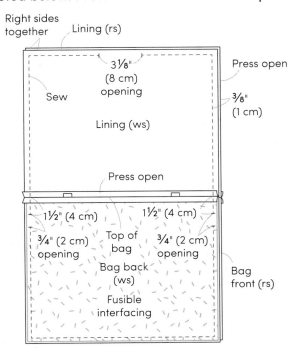

9. To miter the corners on both the bag outside and lining, align each side seam with the bottom seam and sew 2⅜" (6 cm) long seams.

10. Turn right side out through the opening in the lining. Tuck the lining into the bag outside and hand stitch the opening closed. Add two rows of topstitching to create a drawstring casing, following the placement noted below.

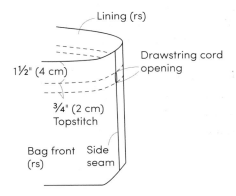

11. Insert the drawstring cords through the openings in opposite directions. Knot the ends of each cord together to form a loop.

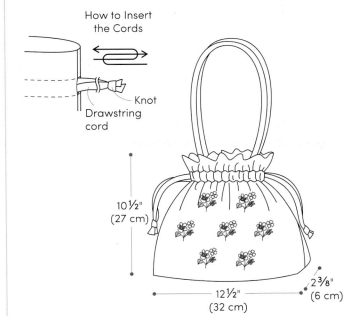

Full-Size Embroidery Template

- Use 3 strands unless otherwise noted
- French knots are wrapped twice

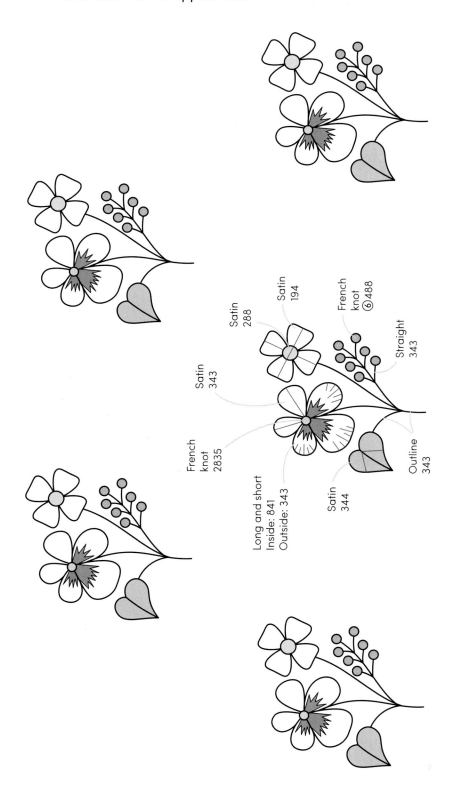

Satin
288

Satin
194

French
knot
⑥488

Satin
343

Straight
343

French
knot
2835

Outline
343

Long and short
Inside: 841
Outside: 343

Satin
344

Full-Size Embroidery Template

- Materials: Olympus No. 25 embroidery floss in 145, 343, 810
- Use 2 strands unless otherwise noted
- Satin stitch unless otherwise noted
- French knots are wrapped twice
- ★ = Straight stitch inside of lazy daisy

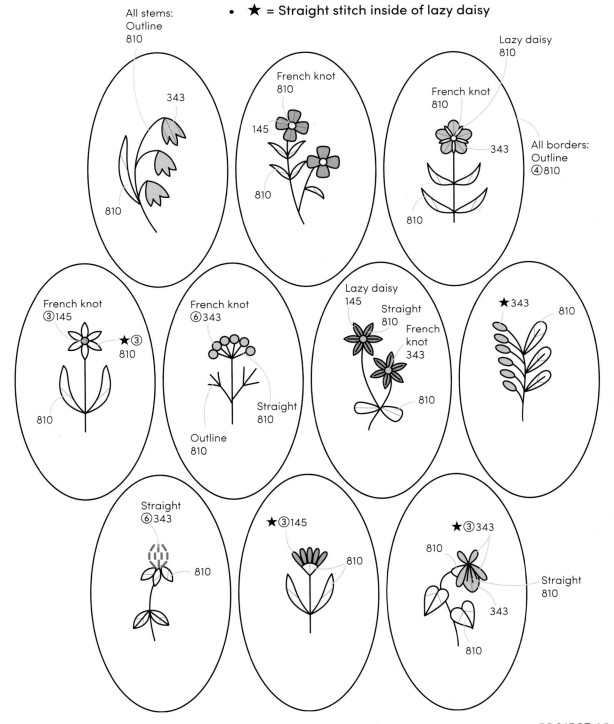

Full-Size Embroidery Templates

- Materials: Olympus No. 25 embroidery floss in 192, 318, 386, 811
- Use 2 strands unless otherwise noted
- Satin stitch unless otherwise noted
- French knots are wrapped twice
- ★ = Straight stitch inside of lazy daisy

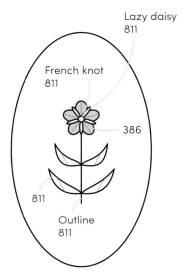

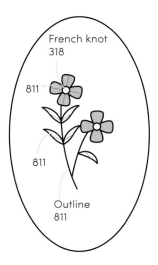

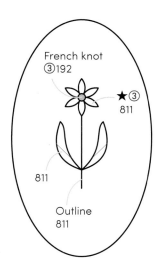

Full-Size Embroidery Template

- Materials: Olympus No. 25 embroidery floss in 421, 484, 486, 792, 2051
- Use 2 strands unless otherwise noted
- Satin stitch unless otherwise noted
- French knots are wrapped twice

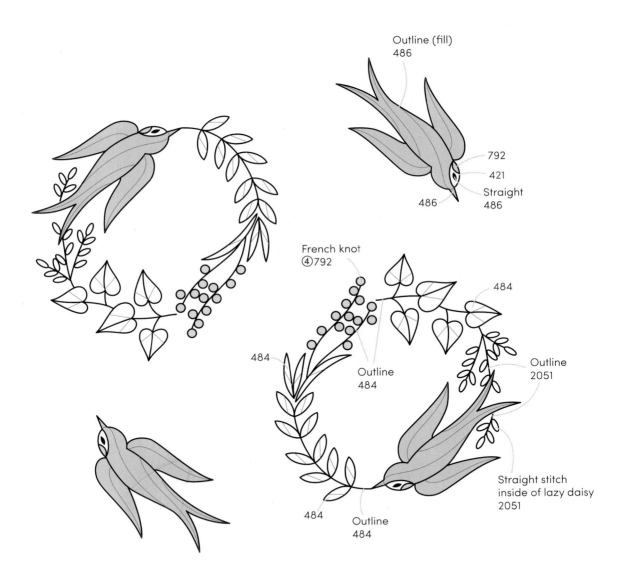

Outline (fill)
486

792
421
Straight
486
486

French knot
④792

484

484

Outline
2051

Outline
484

484

Outline
484

Straight stitch
inside of lazy daisy
2051

08 SHOWN ON PAGE 15

Full-Size Embroidery Template

- Materials: Olympus No. 25 embroidery floss in 201 and 203
- Use Olympus 203 unless otherwise noted
- Use 2 strands unless otherwise noted
- French knots are wrapped twice
- ★ = Straight stitch inside of lazy daisy

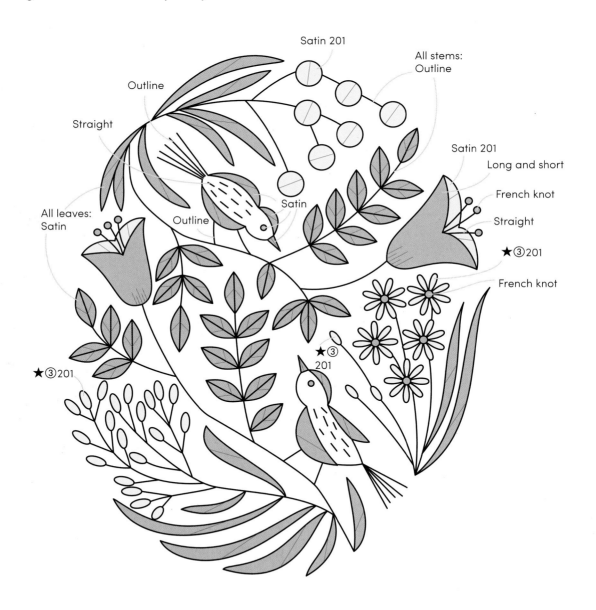

Full-Size Embroidery Template

- Materials: Olympus No. 25 embroidery floss in 284, 288, 486, 758, 783, 792, 795, 2014, 3042, 3043
- Use 2 strands unless otherwise noted
- French knots are wrapped twice

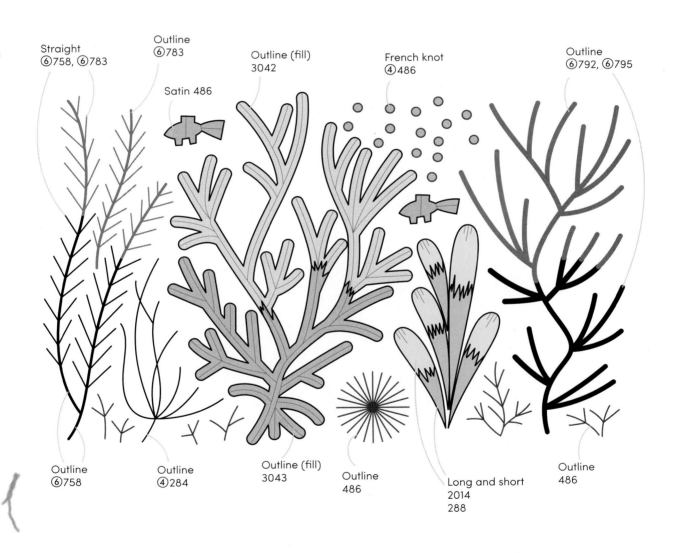

Straight
⑥758, ⑥783

Outline
⑥783

Satin 486

Outline (fill)
3042

French knot
④486

Outline
⑥792, ⑥795

Outline
⑥758

Outline
④284

Outline (fill)
3043

Outline
486

Long and short
2014
288

Outline
486

10

Materials

- ½ yard (0.5 m) of light blue linen fabric (for the bag outside)
- ½ yard (0.5 m) of cotton fabric (for the lining)
- 8" × 6" (20 × 15 cm) of fusible interfacing
- 63" (160 cm) of ⅜" (1 cm) diameter cotton rope
- Olympus No. 25 embroidery floss in 3040

Construction Steps

Use ⅜" (1 cm) seam allowance unless otherwise specified.

1. Cut a 14" × 16¾" (35 × 42 cm) rectangle of light blue linen fabric for the front. Mark an 8" × 10¾" (20 × 27 cm) rectangle for the finished size. You will trim the fabric to size after embroidering. Adhere fusible interfacing to the wrong side in the area where the fabric will be embroidered. Transfer the template on page 74 onto this portion of the fabric, following the placement noted below. Embroider as noted.

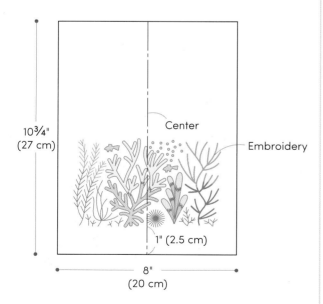

10¾"
(27 cm)

Center

Embroidery

1" (2.5 cm)

8"
(20 cm)

2. Trim the embroidered front to 8¾" × 11½" (22 × 29 cm). These dimensions include seam allowance. Cut another rectangle of light blue linen fabric to this size for the back. Cut two more rectangles of cotton fabric to this size for the lining.

3. Align the embroidered front and one lining with right sides together and sew together along the top. Repeat this step with the bag back and remaining lining.

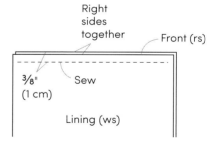

Right sides together

Front (rs)

⅜"
(1 cm)

Sew

Lining (ws)

4. Press the seam allowances open. Align the two units from step 3 with right sides together. Sew together around all four sides, leaving a 3⅛" (8 cm) opening along the bottom of the lining and 1¼" (3 cm) drawstring openings following the placement noted below. Press the seam allowances open.

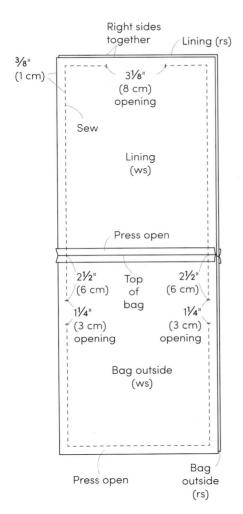

Right sides together

Lining (rs)

⅜" (1 cm)

3⅛" (8 cm) opening

Sew

Lining (ws)

Press open

2½" (6 cm)   Top of bag   2½" (6 cm)

1¼" (3 cm) opening   1¼" (3 cm) opening

Bag outside (ws)

Press open

Bag outside (rs)

5. Turn right side out through the opening in the lining. Hand stitch the opening closed and tuck the lining into the bag outside. Add two rows of topstitching to create a drawstring casing, following the placement noted below.

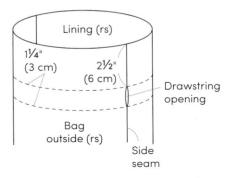

Lining (rs)

1¼" (3 cm)

2½" (6 cm)

Drawstring opening

Bag outside (rs)

Side seam

6. Cut the cotton rope into two 31½" (80 cm) long pieces. Insert through the drawstring openings in opposite directions. Knot the ends of each rope together to form a loop.

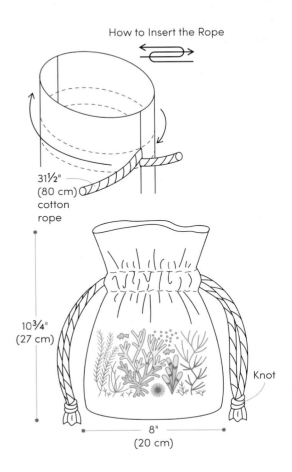

How to Insert the Rope

31½" (80 cm) cotton rope

10¾" (27 cm)

Knot

8" (20 cm)

Full-Size Embroidery Template

- Use Olympus 3040 for all embroidery
- Use 2 strands unless otherwise noted
- French knots are wrapped twice

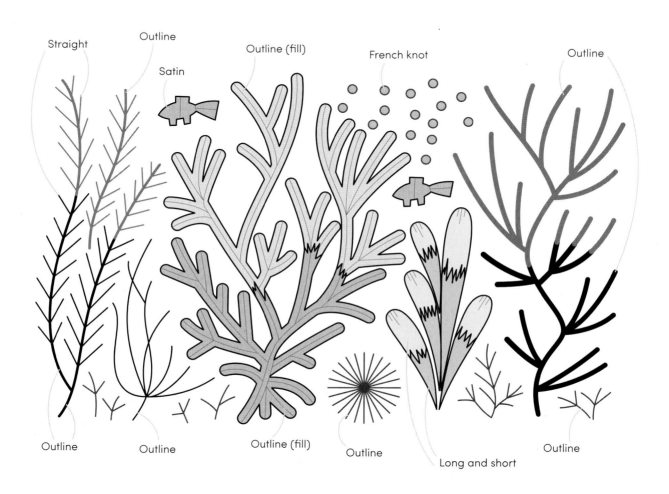

11

Full-Size Embroidery Template

- Materials: Olympus No. 25 embroidery floss in 305, 314, 318
- Use Olympus 305 unless otherwise noted
- Use 2 strands unless otherwise noted
- Use satin stitch unless otherwise noted
- French knots are wrapped twice

12 SHOWN ON PAGE 19 Materials

- ½ yard (0.5 m) of khaki linen fabric
- 3½" × 14" (9 × 35.5 cm) of fusible interfacing
- One set of bell pull hardware with an inner diameter of 4" (10 cm)
- One skein of Olympus No. 25 embroidery floss in 755 (for tassel)
- Olympus No. 25 embroidery floss in 755 and 841

Construction Steps

Use ⅜" (1 cm) seam allowance unless otherwise specified.

---

1. Cut a 14" × 22" (35 × 55.5 cm) rectangle of khaki linen fabric. Mark an 8" × 16" (20 × 40.5 cm) rectangle for the finished size. You will trim the fabric to size after embroidering. Adhere a 3½" × 14" (9 × 35.5 cm) rectangle of fusible interfacing to the wrong side in the area where the fabric will be embroidered. Transfer the templates on page 78 onto this portion of the fabric, following the placement noted below. Embroider as noted. Trim to 8" × 16" (20 × 40.5 cm). These dimensions include seam allowance.

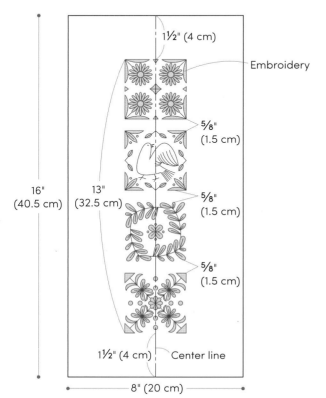

16" (40.5 cm)
13" (32.5 cm)

1½" (4 cm)

Embroidery

⅝" (1.5 cm)

⅝" (1.5 cm)

⅝" (1.5 cm)

1½" (4 cm) — Center line

8" (20 cm)

2. Fold the embroidered fabric in half with right sides together. Sew together along the long edge, leaving a 4" (10 cm) opening.

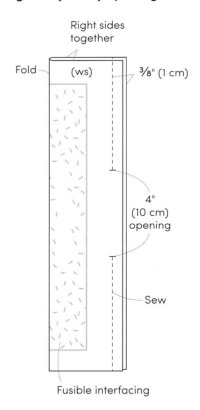

Right sides together

Fold
(ws)
⅜" (1 cm)

4" (10 cm) opening

Sew

Fusible interfacing

3. Press the seam allowance open and turn right side out through the opening. Center the seam along the back and press into shape. Hand stitch the opening closed. Next, fold and press the top and bottom edges over ⅜" (1 cm) and then ⅝" (1.5 cm) toward the back.

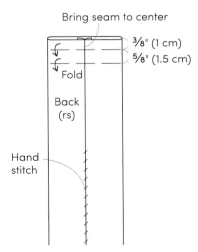

Bring seam to center

⅜" (1 cm)
⅝" (1.5 cm)

Fold

Back (rs)

Hand stitch

4. Hand stitch in place on the back. **Note:** Depending on the type of hardware you use, you may need to insert it onto the embroidered fabric before hand stitching the ends in place.

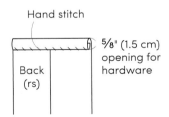

Hand stitch

Back (rs)

⅝" (1.5 cm) opening for hardware

5. Insert the bell pull hardware through the ⅝" (1.5 cm) openings at the top and bottom.

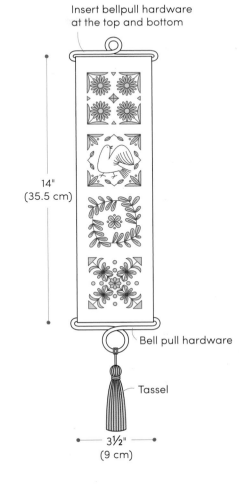

Insert bellpull hardware at the top and bottom

14" (35.5 cm)

Bell pull hardware

Tassel

3½" (9 cm)

How to Make A Tassel

To make A, cut a 4" (10 cm) piece of embroidery floss (all 6 strands). Fold it in half and tie into a loop. To make B, cut a 12" (30 cm) piece of embroidery floss and separate 3 strands.

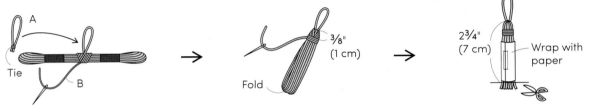

A

Tie

B

⅜" (1 cm)

Fold

2¾" (7 cm)

Wrap with paper

1. Insert the knotted end of A into the center of a skein of embroidery floss with the labels still attached. Wrap B around the skein of floss 6–7 times to secure A in place.

2. Remove the labels and fold the skein of floss in half. Continue wrapping B around the folded skein about ⅜" (1 cm) from the top. Insert the needle through the wraps to secure in place.

3. Cut the loops at the bottom of the tassel. Wrap a piece of paper around the tassel and secure with tape. Trim the bottom as desired.

Full-Size Embroidery Template

- Use Olympus 841 unless otherwise noted
- Use 2 strands unless otherwise noted
- Use satin stitch unless otherwise noted
- French knots are wrapped twice

13

SHOWN ON PAGE 20

Full-Size Embroidery Template

- Materials: Olympus No. 25 embroidery floss in 214, 288, 2014
- Use Olympus 214 unless otherwise noted
- Use 2 strands unless otherwise noted
- Use outline stitch unless otherwise noted
- French knots are wrapped twice
- ★ = Straight stitch inside of lazy daisy

14 SHOWN ON PAGE 21

Materials (for one sachet)

- ⅜ yard (0.4 m) of teal linen fabric
- 6" (15 cm) square of lightweight cotton fabric (for the potpourri bag)
- 4" (10 cm) square of fusible interfacing
- Potpourri
- One skein of Olympus No. 25 embroidery floss in 841 (for the loop)
- Olympus No. 25 embroidery floss in 192, 841, 3041 (small sachet); 222, 841 (medium sachet); 430, 841 (large sachet)

Construction Steps

Use ⅜" (1 cm) seam allowance unless otherwise specified.

1. Cut a rectangle of teal linen fabric according to the dimensions listed in the chart below. Mark the finished size according to the dimensions listed. You will trim the fabric to size after embroidering. Adhere fusible interfacing to the wrong side in the area where the fabric will be embroidered. Transfer the desired template on page 82 onto this portion of the fabric, following the placement noted below. Embroider as noted. Trim along the marked lines.

2. Make the loop: Use three strands of Olympus No. 25 embroidery floss in 841 to work a three-strand braid for 6¼" (16 cm). Tie the braid into a loop.

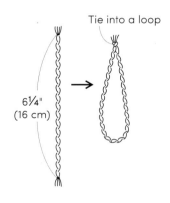

Tie into a loop

6¼" (16 cm)

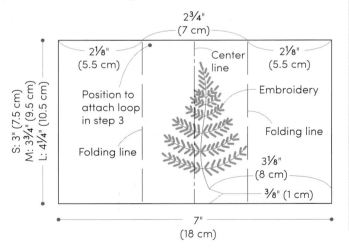

2¾" (7 cm)

2⅛" (5.5 cm)

Center line

2⅛" (5.5 cm)

Position to attach loop in step 3

Embroidery

Folding line

Folding line

3⅛" (8 cm)

⅜" (1 cm)

S: 3" (7.5 cm)
M: 3¾" (9.5 cm)
L: 4¼" (10.5 cm)

7" (18 cm)

	Linen Fabric Cutting Dimensions	Dimensions to Mark Finished Size	Fusible Interfacing Cutting Dimensions
Small	13" × 9" (33 × 22.5 cm)	7" × 3" (18 × 7.5 cm)	2¾" × 2¼" (7 × 5.5 cm)
Medium	13" × 9¾" (33 × 24.5 cm)	7" × 3¾" (18 × 9.5 cm)	2¾" × 3" (7 × 7.5 cm)
Large	13" × 10¼" (33 × 25.5 cm)	7" × 4¼" (18 × 10.5 cm)	2¾" × 3¼" (7 × 8.5 cm)

3. Baste the loop to the right side of the embroidered fabric following the placement noted in the step 1 diagram on page 80.

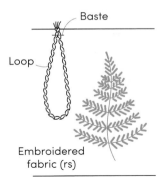

Baste

Loop

Embroidered fabric (rs)

4. Fold and press the left and right edges over ⅜" (1 cm) to the wrong side. Topstitch using ¼" (7 mm) seam allowance to finish the raw edges.

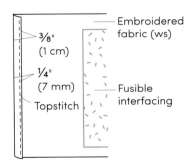

⅜" (1 cm)

¼" (7 mm)

Topstitch

Embroidered fabric (ws)

Fusible interfacing

5. Fold with right sides together along the fold lines noted in the step 1 diagram. This will cause the edges to overlap ¾" (2 cm) at the back. Sew together along the top and bottom. Turn right side out.

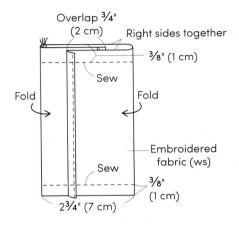

Overlap ¾" (2 cm)

Right sides together

⅜" (1 cm)

Sew

Fold

Fold

Embroidered fabric (ws)

Sew

⅜" (1 cm)

2¾" (7 cm)

6. Cut a rectangle of lightweight cotton fabric for the potpourri bag according to the dimensions listed in the chart below. Fold in half with right sides together. Sew together along the side and bottom using ¼" (5 mm) seam allowance.

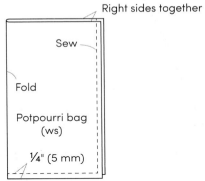

Right sides together

Sew

Fold

Potpourri bag (ws)

¼" (5 mm)

Potpourri Bag Cutting Dimensions

Small	5½" × 3¼" (14 × 8.5 cm)
Medium	5½" × 4¼" (14 × 11 cm)
Large	5½" × 4¾" (14 × 12 cm)

7. Turn right side out. Fill with potpourri. Fold the top over and insert into the embroidered sachet. **Note:** Leaving the potpourri bag unsewn along the top will allow you to easily change out the potpourri as desired. If you are worried about the potpourri spilling out, hand stitch the top closed.

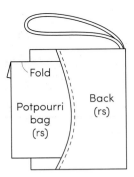

Fold

Back (rs)

Potpourri bag (rs)

Full-Size Embroidery Templates

- Use 2 strands unless otherwise noted
- Use outline stitch unless otherwise noted
- French knots are wrapped twice
- ★ = Straight stitch inside of lazy daisy

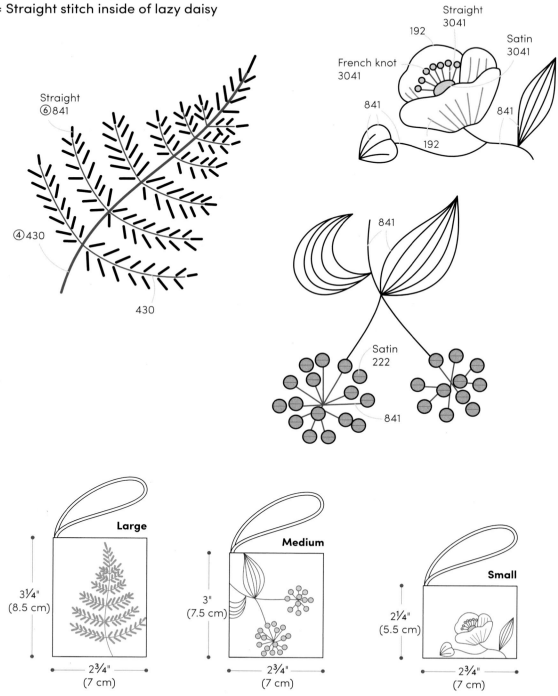

15

SHOWN ON PAGE 22

Full-Size Embroidery Template

- Materials: Olympus No. 25 embroidery floss in 218, 288, 342, 575, 632, 712, 785, 2835
- Use 2 strands unless otherwise noted
- Use outline stitch unless otherwise noted
- French knots are wrapped twice
- ★ = Straight stitch inside of lazy daisy
- △ = Long and short stitch in 218   ● = Satin stitch in 218

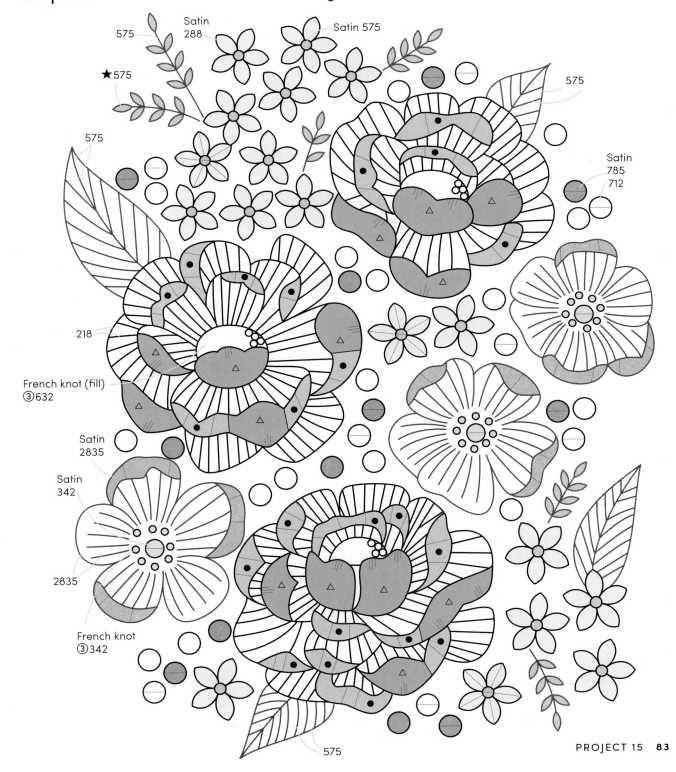

Satin 288
575
Satin 575
★575
575
575
575
Satin 785 712
218
French knot (fill) ③632
Satin 2835
Satin 342
2835
French knot ③342
575

16

SHOWN ON PAGE 23

Full-Size Embroidery Template

- Materials: Olympus No. 25 embroidery floss in 412, 485, 631, 741, 841, 2051, 3042, 7020
- Use 2 strands unless otherwise noted
- Use outline stitch unless otherwise noted
- French knots are wrapped twice
- ★ = Straight stitch inside of lazy daisy
- △ = Long and short stitch in 3042   ● = Satin stitch in 3042

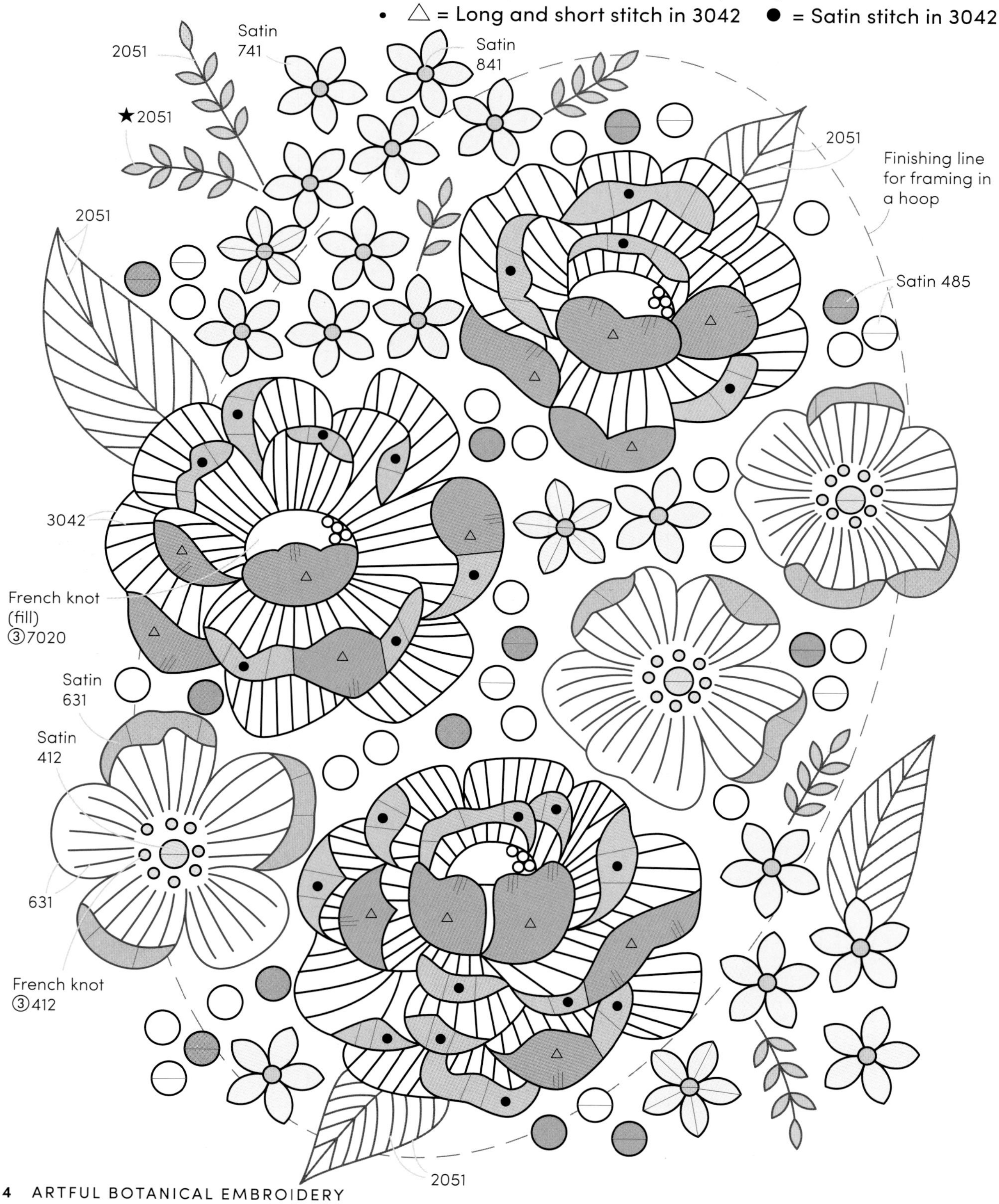

2051

Satin 741

Satin 841

★2051

2051

Finishing line for framing in a hoop

2051

Satin 485

3042

French knot (fill) ③7020

Satin 631

Satin 412

631

French knot ③412

2051

17 SHOWN ON PAGE 24

Full-Size Embroidery Template

- Materials: Olympus No. 25 embroidery floss in 755 and 841
- Use Olympus 841 unless otherwise noted
- Use 3 strands unless otherwise noted
- Use satin stitch unless otherwise noted

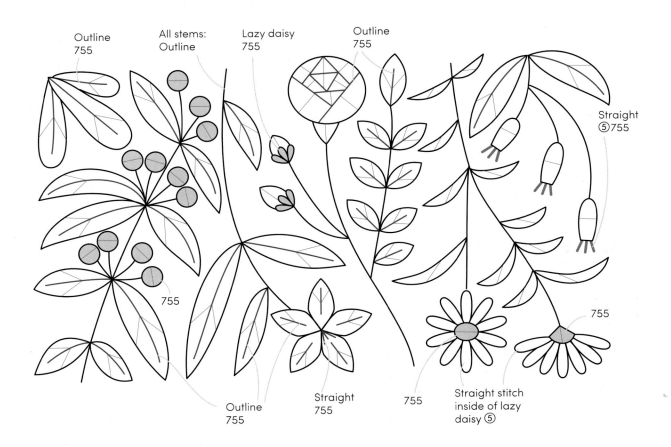

18

SHOWN ON PAGE 25

Materials

- ½ yard (0.5 m) of pink linen fabric (for the bag outside)
- ½ yard (0.5 m) of linen fabric (for the lining)
- 17¾" × 11¾" (45 × 30 cm) of fusible interfacing
- Olympus No. 25 embroidery floss in 744 and 778

Construction Steps

Use ⅜" (1 cm) seam allowance unless otherwise specified.

1. Cut a 13½" × 15" (34 × 38 cm) rectangle of pink linen fabric for the front. Mark a 7½" × 9" (19 × 23 cm) rectangle for the finished size. You will trim the fabric to size after embroidering. Adhere a 8¼" × 9¾" (21 × 25 cm) rectangle of fusible interfacing to the wrong side. Transfer the template on page 88 onto the fabric, following the placement noted below. Embroider as noted.

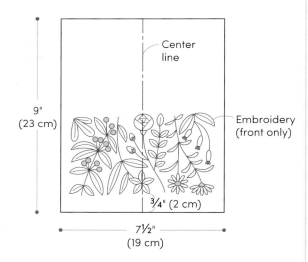

Center line

9" (23 cm)

Embroidery (front only)

¾" (2 cm)

7½" (19 cm)

2. Trim the embroidered front to 8¼" × 9¾" (21 × 25 cm). These dimensions include seam allowance. Cut another rectangle of pink linen fabric to this size for the back. Adhere fusible interfacing to the wrong side of the back. Cut two more rectangles of linen fabric to this size for the lining.

3. Cut two 15" × 1½" (38 × 4 cm) rectangles of pink linen fabric for the handles.

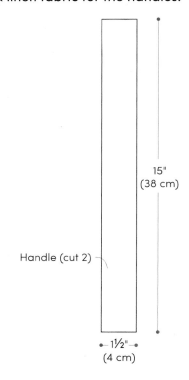

15" (38 cm)

Handle (cut 2)

1½" (4 cm)

4. To make each handle, fold and press each long edge in ⅜" (1 cm). Then, fold the handle in half and press. Topstitch, stitching as close to the edge as possible.

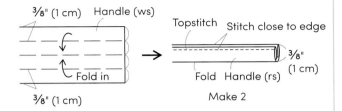

5. Baste one handle to the right side of the bag front following the placement noted below. Baste the other handle to the right side of the bag back.

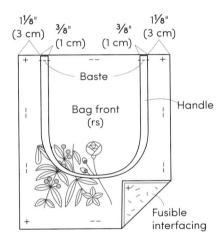

6. Align the bag front and one lining with right sides together and sew along the top. Repeat this step with the bag back and remaining lining.

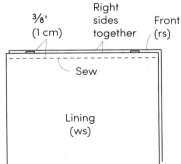

7. Press the seam allowances open. Align the two units from step 6 with right sides together. Sew around all four sides, leaving a 3⅛" (8 cm) opening along the bottom of the lining. Press the seam allowances open.

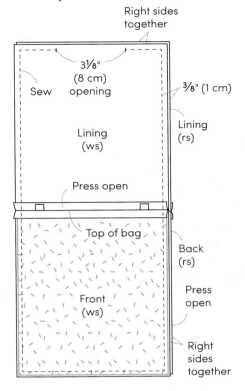

8. Turn right side out through the opening in the lining. Hand stitch the opening closed and tuck the lining into the bag outside.

Full-Size Embroidery Template

- Use Olympus 744 unless otherwise noted
- Use 3 strands unless otherwise noted
- Use satin stitch unless otherwise noted

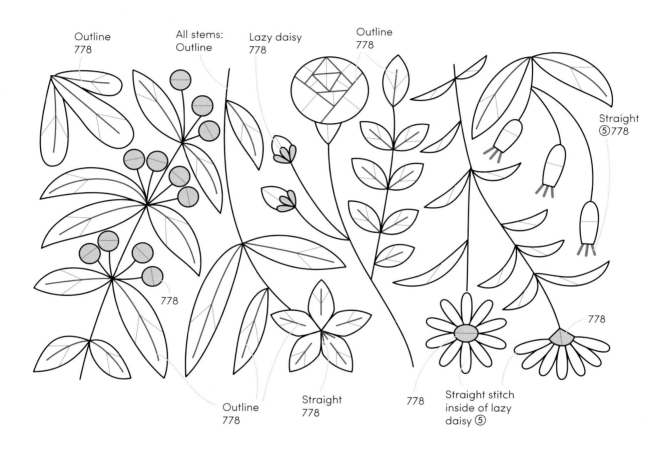

Outline 778

All stems: Outline

Lazy daisy 778

Outline 778

Straight ⑤778

778

778

Outline 778

Straight 778

778

Straight stitch inside of lazy daisy ⑤

19

SHOWN ON PAGE 26

Full-Size Embroidery Template

- Materials: Olympus No. 25 embroidery floss in 575, 632, 841, 2835, 3043
- Use 2 strands unless otherwise noted
- French knots are wrapped twice
- ★ = Straight stitch inside of lazy daisy

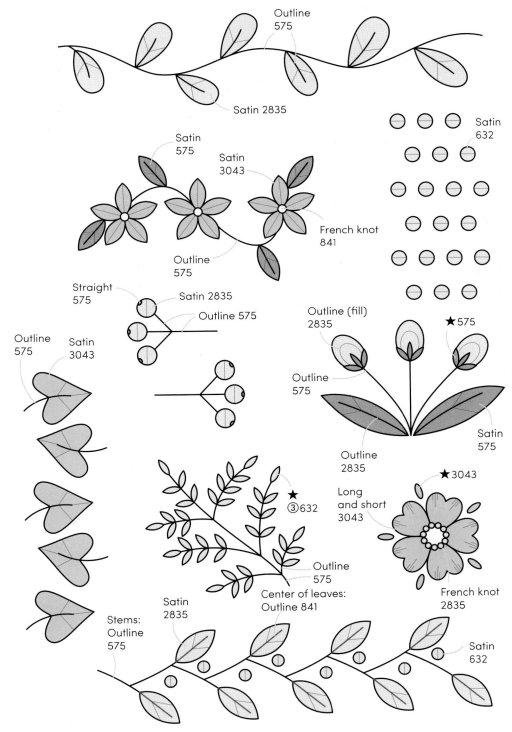

Outline 575

Satin 2835

Satin 575

Satin 3043

Satin 632

Outline 575

French knot 841

Straight 575

Satin 2835

Outline 575

Outline (fill) 2835

★575

Outline 575

Satin 3043

Outline 575

Outline 575

Satin 575

Outline 2835

Long and short 3043

★3043

★③632

Outline 575

Center of leaves: Outline 841

French knot 2835

Stems: Outline 575

Satin 2835

Satin 632

20

SHOWN ON PAGE 27

Materials

- ½ yard (0.5 m) of light blue linen fabric (for the patchwork and bag outside)
- ¼ yard (0.3 m) of black linen fabric (for the patchwork)
- ¼ yard (0.3 m) of beige linen fabric (for the patchwork)
- ½ yard (0.5 m) of linen fabric (for the lining)
- 9¾" × 17¾" (25 × 45 cm) of fusible fleece
- 21¾" × 23¾" (55 × 60 cm) of fusible interfacing
- 27½" (70 cm) of ⅛" (3 mm) diameter braided leather cord
- Olympus No. 25 embroidery floss in 222, 755, 841

Construction Steps

Use ⅜" (1 cm) seam allowance unless otherwise specified.

1. Adhere fusible interfacing to the wrong side of each color of linen fabric to be used for the patchwork. Cut pieces into 6" (15 cm) squares and transfer the templates on page 92 onto the fabric. Embroider as noted. Trim each embroidered piece to the dimensions noted in the chart below, then sew together following the numerical order noted below.

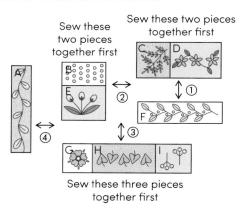

Sew these two pieces together first

Sew these two pieces together first

Sew these three pieces together first

2. Trim the assembled flap to 8¾" × 5½" (22 × 14 cm). These dimensions include seam allowance.

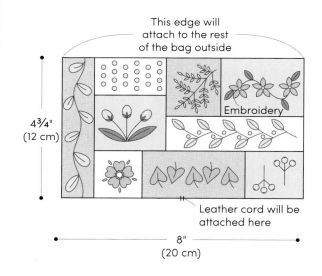

This edge will attach to the rest of the bag outside

Embroidery

4¾" (12 cm)

Leather cord will be attached here

8" (20 cm)

Piece	Trimming Dimensions (Includes Seam Allowance)	Piece	Trimming Dimensions (Includes Seam Allowance)
A	1¾" × 5½" (4.7 × 14 cm)	F	2" × 5¼" (5 × 13.3 cm)
B	2" × 3¼" (5.2 × 8 cm)	G	2¼" × 2½" (6 × 6 cm)
C	2¾" × 2½" (7 × 6.5 cm)	H	2¼" × 4" (6 × 10.5 cm)
D	2¾" × 3½" (7 × 8.8 cm)	I	2¼" × 2¾" (6 × 6.8 cm)
E	2¾" × 3¼" (6.8 × 8 cm)		

3. Cut a 8¾" × 11" (22 × 28 cm) rectangle of light blue linen fabric. These dimensions include seam allowance. Adhere fusible interfacing to the wrong side. Sew the top edge to the flap with right sides together. This will be the bag outside.

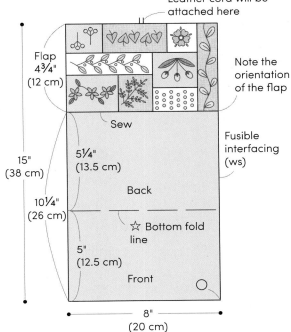

Leather cord will be attached here

Flap 4¾" (12 cm)

Note the orientation of the flap

15" (38 cm)

5¼" (13.5 cm)

Sew

Fusible interfacing (ws)

Back

10¼" (26 cm)

☆ Bottom fold line

5" (12.5 cm)

Front

8" (20 cm)

4. Baste the 27½" (70 cm) leather cord to the top center of the flap along the seam allowance. Cut a 8¾" × 15¾" (22 × 40 cm) rectangle of linen fabric for the lining and a 8" × 15" (20 × 38 cm) rectangle of fusible fleece. Adhere the fusible fleece to the wrong side of the lining. Next, align the bag outside and lining with right sides together and sew along the bottom, leaving a 3⅛" (8 cm) opening.

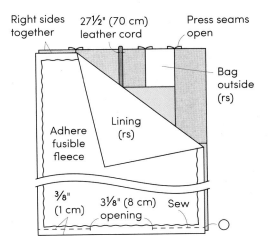

Right sides together

27½" (70 cm) leather cord

Press seams open

Bag outside (rs)

Adhere fusible fleece

Lining (rs)

⅜" (1 cm)

3⅛" (8 cm) opening

Sew

5. Fold along the ☆, bringing the seam sewn in step 4 (○) in 5" (12.5 cm) from the bottom edge. Sew together along three sides, and then turn right side out through the opening in the lining.

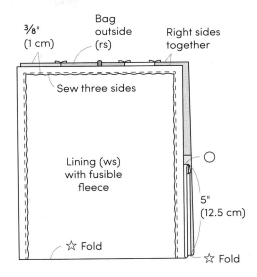

⅜" (1 cm)

Bag outside (rs)

Right sides together

Sew three sides

Lining (ws) with fusible fleece

5" (12.5 cm)

☆ Fold

☆ Fold

6. Hand stitch the opening closed and tuck the lining into the bag outside.

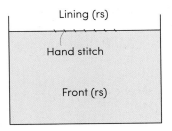

Lining (rs)

Hand stitch

Front (rs)

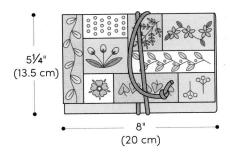

5¼" (13.5 cm)

8" (20 cm)

Full-Size Embroidery Template

- Use 2 strands unless otherwise noted
- French knots are wrapped twice
- ★ = Straight stitch inside of lazy daisy

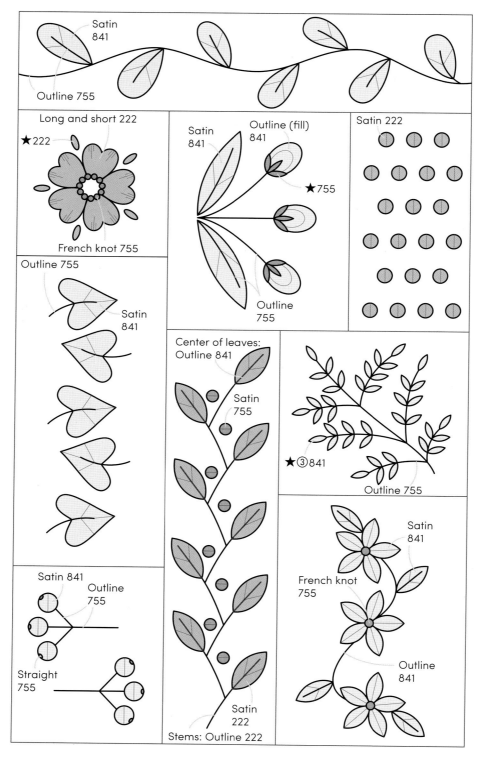

Satin 841

Outline 755

Long and short 222

★222

French knot 755

Outline 755

Satin 841

Satin 841

Outline (fill) 841

★755

Outline 755

Satin 222

Center of leaves: Outline 841

Satin 755

★③841

Outline 755

Satin 841

Outline 755

Straight 755

Satin 222

Stems: Outline 222

Satin 841

French knot 755

Outline 841

21

Full-Size Embroidery Template

- Materials: Olympus No. 25 embroidery floss in 841 and 1035
- Use 2 strands unless otherwise noted
- Bullion knots are wrapped five times

Bullion knot
④841

Satin
1035

Straight stitch
inside of lazy
daisy 1035

Outline
1035

22

SHOWN ON PAGE 29

Materials

- ½ yard (0.5 m) of yellow rayon/cotton satin fabric (for the outside)
- ½ yard (0.5 m) of cotton fabric (for the lining)
- 71" (180 cm) of ⅛" (3 mm) diameter cord
- Olympus No. 25 embroidery floss in 841 and 2835

Construction Steps

Use ⅜" (1 cm) seam allowance unless otherwise specified.

1. Cut a 15¾" × 14" (40 × 35 cm) rectangle of yellow rayon/cotton satin fabric for the front. Mark a 9¾" × 8" (25 × 20 cm) rectangle for the finished size. You will trim the fabric to size after embroidering. Transfer the template on page 96 onto the fabric following the placement noted below. Embroider as noted.

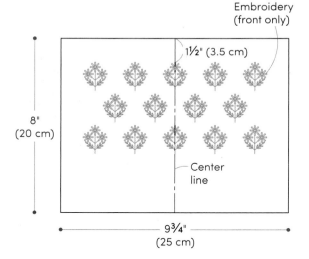

Embroidery (front only)

1½" (3.5 cm)

8" (20 cm)

Center line

9¾" (25 cm)

Note

If using a stiff fabric like the rayon/cotton satin pictured in the sample on page 29, there's no need to adhere fusible interfacing, but if using a lightweight fabric, such as linen, make sure to adhere fusible interfacing to the wrong side in the area where the fabric will be embroidered.

2. Trim the embroidered front to 10½" × 8¾" (27 × 22 cm). These dimensions include seam allowance. Cut another rectangle of yellow rayon/cotton satin fabric to this size for the back. Cut two more rectangles of cotton fabric to this size for the lining.

3. Align the embroidered front and one lining with right sides together and sew together along the top. Repeat this step with the back and remaining lining.

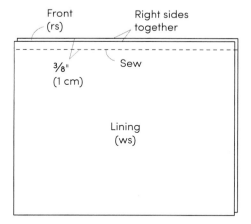

Front (rs)

Right sides together

⅜" (1 cm)

Sew

Lining (ws)

4. Press the seam allowances open. Align the two units from step 3 with right sides together. Sew together around all four sides, leaving a 2½" (6 cm) opening along the bottom of the lining and ¾" (2 cm) drawstring openings following the placement noted below. Press the seam allowances open.

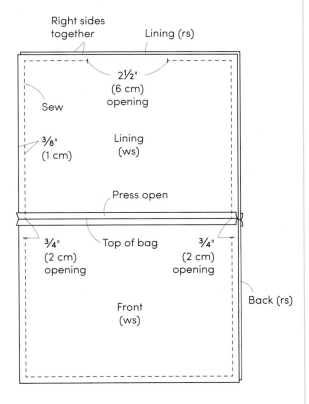

5. To miter the corners on both the bag outside and lining, align each side seam with the bottom seam and sew 4" (10 cm) long seams. Trim the excess fabric, leaving ⅜" (1 cm) seam allowance.

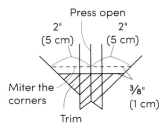

6. Turn right side out through the opening in the lining. Hand stitch the opening closed and tuck the lining into the bag outside. Topstitch ¾" (2 cm) from the top of the bag to create a drawstring casing. Cut the cord into two 35½" (90 cm) pieces. Insert the drawstring cord through the openings in opposite directions. Knot the ends of each cord together to form a loop.

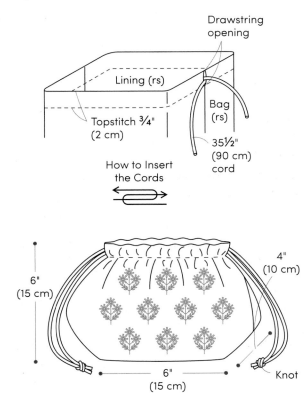

Full-Size Embroidery Template

- Use 2 strands unless otherwise noted
- Bullion knots are wrapped five times

Bullion knot
④ 2835

Satin
841

Outline
2835

Straight
stitch
inside of
lazy daisy
2835

Full-Size Embroidery Template

- Materials: Olympus No. 25 embroidery floss in 198, 218, 343, 344, 488, 563, 738, 785, 841, 1029, 2835
- Use 2 strands unless otherwise noted
- French knots are wrapped twice

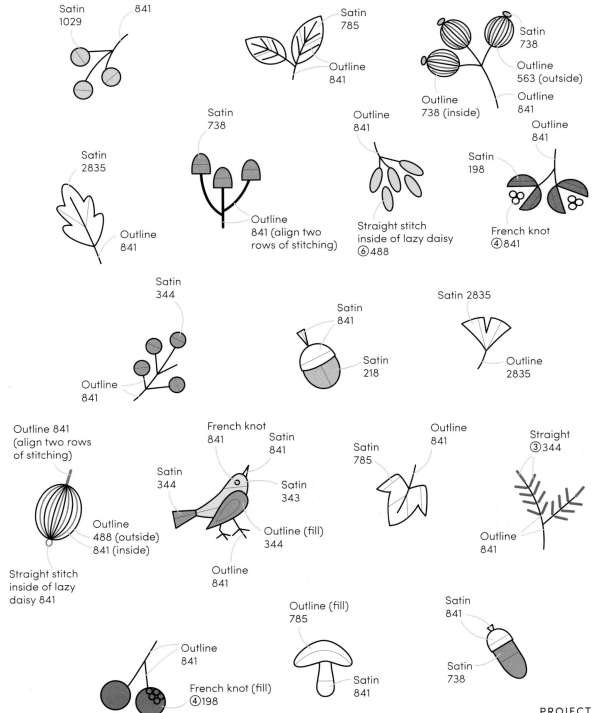

Full-Size Embroidery Templates

- Materials: Olympus No. 25 embroidery floss in 222, 244, 755, 2051
- Use 2 strands unless otherwise noted
- French knots are wrapped twice

Satin
755

Outline
2051

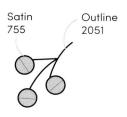

Satin
755

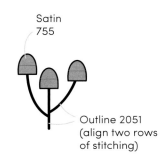

Outline 2051
(align two rows
of stitching)

Satin
222

Outline
244

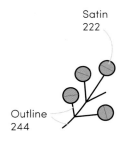

French
knot
222

Satin
222

Satin
222

Satin
244

Outline (fill)
222

Outline
222

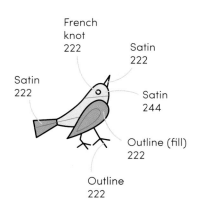

Outline (fill)
755

Satin
2051

Full-Size Embroidery Template

- Materials: Olympus No. 25 embroidery floss in 192, 810, 900
- Use 3 strands unless otherwise noted
- French knots are wrapped twice

Satin
192

French knot
900

Outline (align two
rows of stitching)
900

Satin 900

Blanket
192

Center of leaves:
Outline 810

Outline
900

Materials

- ½ yard (0.5 m) of blue linen fabric (for the outside)
- ½ yard (0.5 m) of cotton fabric (for the lining)
- 9¾" × 11¾" (25 × 30 cm) of fusible interfacing
- One 8" (20 cm) zipper
- One skein of Olympus No. 25 embroidery floss in 318 (for the tassel)
- Olympus No. 25 embroidery floss in 810, 900, 3043
- Polyester stuffing (for the pin cushion)

Construction Steps

Use ⅜" (1 cm) seam allowance unless otherwise specified.

---

1. Cut a 13" × 10¾" (33 × 27 cm) rectangle of blue linen fabric for the front. Mark a 7" × 4¾" (18 × 12 cm) rectangle for the finished size. You will trim the fabric to size after embroidering. Adhere fusible interfacing to the wrong side. Transfer the template on page 101 onto the fabric, following the placement noted below. Embroider as noted.

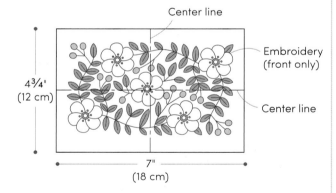

Center line

Embroidery (front only)

Center line

4¾" (12 cm)

7" (18 cm)

2. Trim the embroidered front to 7¾" × 5½" (20 × 14 cm). These dimensions include seam allowance. Cut another rectangle of blue linen fabric to this size for the back. Cut two more rectangles of cotton fabric to this size for the lining.

3. Stitch across the zipper tape 6½" (16.5 cm) from the top stop, then trim the excess, leaving ¾" (2 cm) seam allowance from the stitching.

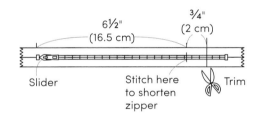

6½" (16.5 cm)

¾" (2 cm)

Slider

Stitch here to shorten zipper

Trim

4. With right sides together, sew the zipper to the embroidered front along the top edge, positioning the zipper as shown below.

⅝" (1.5 cm) Fold ends of zipper

¼" (5 mm) Sew

Right sides together

Zipper (ws)

Front (rs)

5. Next, align one of the lining pieces on top with the wrong side facing up. Sew together along the top. Repeat steps 4 and 5 to sew the other half of the zipper to the back and remaining lining piece.

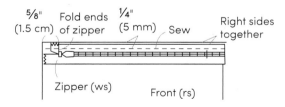

¼" (7 mm)

Right sides together

Front (rs)

Sew

Lining (ws)

6. Open flat, aligning the two linings and two bag outsides with right sides together. Sew together around all four sides, leaving a 2½" (6 cm) opening along the bottom of the lining.

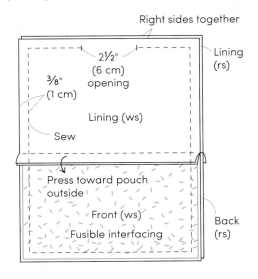

Right sides together

Lining (rs)

2½" (6 cm) opening

⅜" (1 cm)

Lining (ws)

Sew

Press toward pouch outside

Front (ws)

Fusible interfacing

Back (rs)

7. Turn right side out through the opening in the lining. Hand stitch the opening closed and tuck the lining into the bag outside.

8. Make a tassel as shown on page 77 and attach it to the zipper slider.

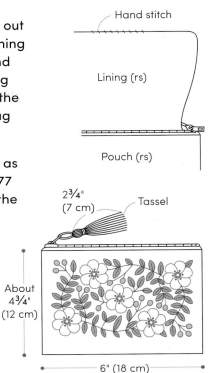

Hand stitch

Lining (rs)

Pouch (rs)

2¾" (7 cm)

Tassel

About 4¾" (12 cm)

6" (18 cm)

Full-Size Embroidery Template

- Use 3 strands unless otherwise noted
- French knots are wrapped twice

Satin 810

French knot 900

Outline (align two rows of stitching) 900

Satin 900

Blanket 810

Center of leaves: Outline 3043

Outline 900

FOR THE PIN CUSHION

Use ⅜" (1 cm) seam allowance unless otherwise specified.

1. Cut a 7" (18 cm) square of blue linen fabric for the front. Mark a 3¾" (9.5 cm) square for the finished size. You will trim the fabric to size after embroidering. Adhere fusible interfacing to the wrong side. Transfer the below template onto the fabric. Embroider as noted. Trim the embroidered front to 4½" (11.5 cm) square.

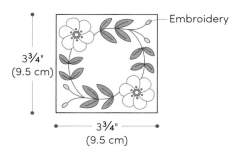

2. Cut two 2½" × 4½" (6.7 × 11.5 cm) rectangles of blue linen for the back. These measurements include seam allowance.

3. Align the two back pieces with right sides together. Sew along one long edge, leaving a 1½" (4 cm) opening at the center. Press the seam allowance open. Align the assembled back with the embroidered front. Sew together around all four sides.

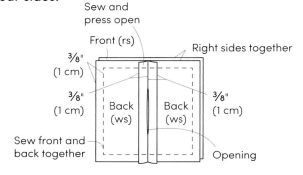

4. Turn right side out through the opening. Fill with polyester stuffing and hand stitch the opening closed.

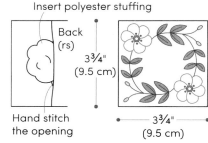

Full-Size Embroidery Template

- Use 3 strands unless otherwise noted
- French knots are wrapped twice

Full-Size Embroidery Template

- Materials: Olympus No. 25 embroidery floss in 145, 192, 288, 290, 318, 343, 393, 623, 841, 900, 2014, 2835
- Use 3 strands unless otherwise noted
- French knots are wrapped twice

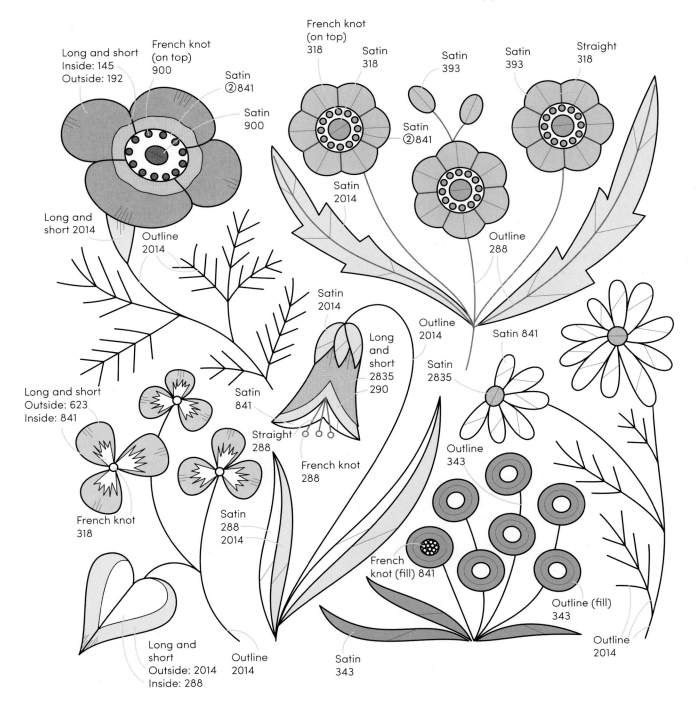

Full-Size Embroidery Template

- Materials: Olympus No. 25 embroidery floss in 137, 202, 205, 318, 342, 841, 843, 1601, 1904, 1906
- Use 2 strands unless otherwise noted
- French knots are wrapped twice
- ★ = Straight stitch inside of lazy daisy

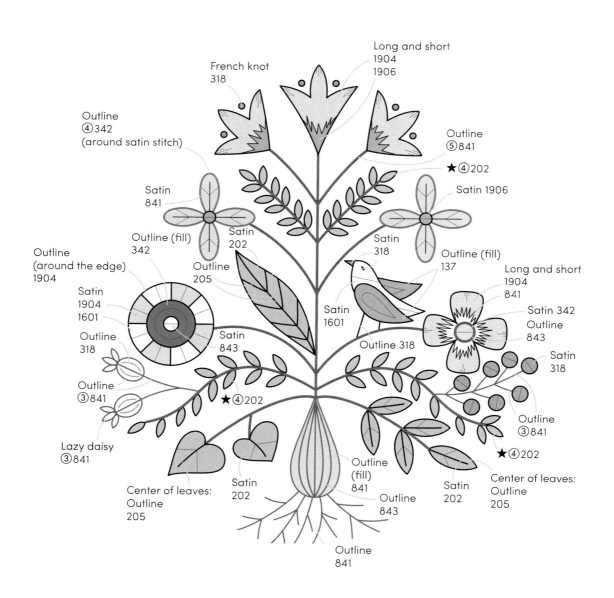

French knot
318

Long and short
1904
1906

Outline
④342
(around satin stitch)

Outline
⑤841

★④202

Satin
841

Satin 1906

Outline (fill)
342

Satin
202

Satin
318

Outline (fill)
137

Long and short
1904
841

Outline
(around the edge)
1904

Outline
205

Satin 342

Satin
1904
1601

Outline
843

Outline
318

Satin
843

Satin
1601

Satin
318

Outline
③841

Outline 318

Outline
③841

Lazy daisy
③841

★④202

★④202

Center of leaves:
Outline
205

Satin
202

Outline
(fill)
841

Satin
202

Center of leaves:
Outline
205

Outline
843

Outline
841

Full-Size Embroidery Template

- Materials: Olympus No. 25 embroidery floss in 758 and 841
- Use 3 strands of 758 unless otherwise noted
- Use outline stitch unless otherwise noted
- French knots are wrapped twice
- ★ = Straight stitch inside of lazy daisy

Full-Size Embroidery Template

- Materials: Olympus No. 25 embroidery floss in 318 and 841
- Use 3 strands of 318 unless otherwise noted
- Use outline stitch unless otherwise noted
- French knots are wrapped twice
- ★ = Straight stitch inside of lazy daisy

Materials

- 6" × 11¾" (15 × 30 cm) of gray linen fabric
- 2½" × 8" (6 × 20 cm) of fusible interfacing
- Olympus No. 25 embroidery floss in 318, 421, 654, 655, 2042, 2835

Construction Steps

Use ⅜" (1 cm) seam allowance unless otherwise specified.

1. Cut a 6" × 11¾" (15 × 30 cm) rectangle of gray linen fabric. Mark a 3⅛" × 8½" (8 × 21.5 cm) rectangle for the finished size. You will trim the fabric to size after embroidering. Adhere fusible interfacing to the wrong side in the area where the fabric will be embroidered. Transfer the desired template on page 109 onto the fabric, following the placement noted below. Make sure to transfer the bookmark outline as well. Embroider as noted.

2. Trim the embroidered fabric to 3⅛" × 8½" (8 × 21.5 cm). These dimensions include seam allowance. Fold in half with right sides together. Sew together along the long edge, leaving a 2½" (6 cm) opening.

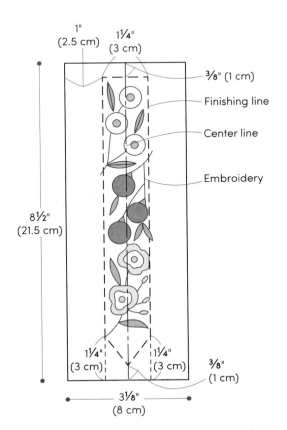

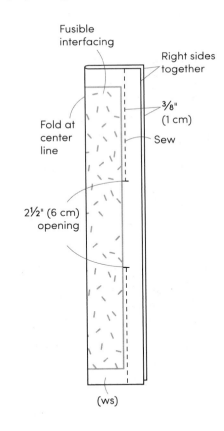

3. Center the seam and press open. Sew across the top using ⅜" (1 cm) seam allowance. Next, sew along the bottom point following the outline of the bookmark traced onto the fabric in step 1. Trim the excess fabric at the bottom, leaving a V-shaped seam allowance as shown below.

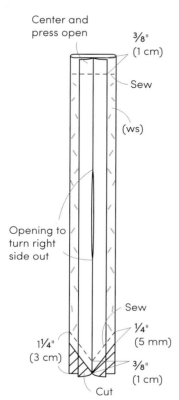

Center and press open

⅜"
(1 cm)

Sew

(ws)

Opening to turn right side out

Sew

¼"
(5 mm)

1¼"
(3 cm)

⅜"
(1 cm)

Cut

4. Turn right side out through the opening. Adjust the shape, then hand stitch the opening closed.

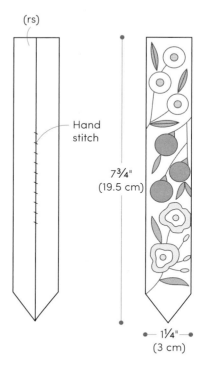

(rs)

Hand stitch

7¾"
(19.5 cm)

1¼"
(3 cm)

Full-Size Embroidery Templates

- Use 2 strands unless otherwise noted
- French knots are wrapped twice
- ★ = Straight stitch inside of lazy daisy

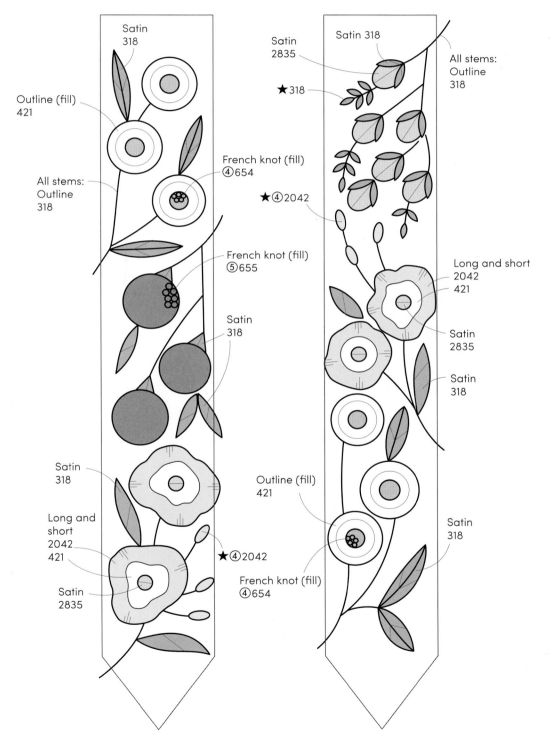

Full-Size Embroidery Template

- Materials: Olympus No. 25 embroidery floss in 305 and 316
- Use 3 strands of 305 unless otherwise noted
- Use satin stitch unless otherwise noted
- French knots are wrapped twice
- ★ = Straight stitch inside of lazy daisy

★⑥316

Outline 316

★316

Outline 316

316

Outline

316

Outline 316

Outline 316

316

French knot

Outline 316

Satin

Outline

Outline 316

Long and short

Outline

Long and short

★⑥

Full-Size Embroidery Template

- Materials: Olympus No. 25 embroidery floss in 145 and 192
- Use 2 strands of 192 unless otherwise noted
- Use outline stitch unless otherwise noted
- French knots are wrapped twice

Embroidery Stitch Guide

All of the designs in this book were made with basic embroidery stitches. Use the handy guide below as a quick reference when stitching.

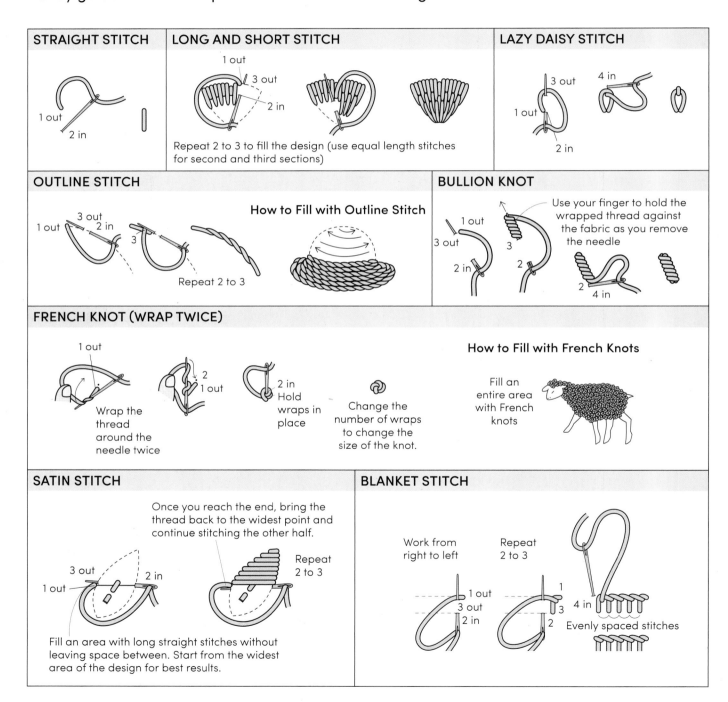

STRAIGHT STITCH

1 out
2 in

LONG AND SHORT STITCH

1 out
3 out
2 in

Repeat 2 to 3 to fill the design (use equal length stitches for second and third sections)

LAZY DAISY STITCH

3 out
4 in
1 out
2 in

OUTLINE STITCH

1 out
3 out
2 in
3

How to Fill with Outline Stitch

Repeat 2 to 3

BULLION KNOT

1 out
3 out
3
2 in
2
2
4 in

Use your finger to hold the wrapped thread against the fabric as you remove the needle

FRENCH KNOT (WRAP TWICE)

1 out

Wrap the thread around the needle twice

2
1 out

2 in
Hold wraps in place

Change the number of wraps to change the size of the knot.

How to Fill with French Knots

Fill an entire area with French knots

SATIN STITCH

Once you reach the end, bring the thread back to the widest point and continue stitching the other half.

3 out
1 out
2 in

Repeat 2 to 3

Fill an area with long straight stitches without leaving space between. Start from the widest area of the design for best results.

BLANKET STITCH

Work from right to left

Repeat 2 to 3

1 out
3 out
2 in

1
3
2

4 in

Evenly spaced stitches